READING SHAKESPEARE'S PLAYS

By GEORGE R. PRICE

Department of English
Michigan State University

BARRON'S EDUCATIONAL SERIES

Woodbury, New York

FOREWORD

THIS manual is intended to be used by students of courses in which the text of Shakespeare is in the form either of editions of single plays or of an edition of the complete works which is not equipped with a general introduction on the topics included herein. The substance of these chapters I consider to be the minimum that an undergraduate should study and employ as background for the understanding of the plays. No sketch of the Elizabethan drama is offered, for my impression is that such a chapter presents the ordinary undergraduate with a discouraging succession of unfamiliar names of dramatists and plays and of meaningless dates. Furthermore, because of the fact that almost all editions prefix to each play an introduction reciting the evidence for its date and sources, I omit that material from this guide. I also omit extended critical discussion of individual plays, that being the province of the instructor. However, for the benefit of students who wish to supplement the instructor's interpretation, a few titles of critical works are cited below.

In teaching Shakespeare for many years I have assimilated as much information as I could from the legion of Shakespeare scholars past and present, with the result that often it is no longer possible for me to name the book or article to which I am originally indebted for facts or interpretations. This statement may explain, if it does not excuse, the rarity of footnotes in the book. However, for purposes of checking details and supplementing my information, I have consulted the following authorities, besides some that are cited in footnotes to the chapters:

CHAPTER II: C. Walter Hodges, *The Globe Restored*, 1954, and "Unworthy Scaffolds: A Theory for the Reconstruction of Elizabethan Playhouses," *Shakespeare Survey*, III (1950), 83-94; Richard Hosley, "The Gallery Over the Stage in the Public Playhouse," *Shakespeare Quarterly*, VIII (1957), 15-31; Richard Southern, "On Reconstructing a Practicable Elizabethan Public Playhouse," *Shakespeare Survey*, XII (1959), 22-34; Alfred Harbage, *Shakespeare's Audience*, 1941.

CHAPTER III: Lawrence Babb, *The Elizabethan Malady*, 1951; Paul Kocher, *Science and Religion in Elizabethan England*, 1953.

CHAPTER IV: E. K. Chambers, *William Shakespeare*, 1930, and *Sources for a Biography of Shakespeare*, 1946; T. W. Baldwin, *William Shakspere's Small Latine & Lesse Greeke*, I (1944); James G. McManaway, "Recent Studies in Shakespeare's Chronology," *Shakespeare Survey*, III (1950), 22-33.

CHAPTER V: E. K. Chambers, *William Shakespeare*, 1930; Charles T. Prouty, "Introduction," *Mr. William Shakespeares Comedies, Histories, & Tragedies*, 1954.

In this book my references to lines in the plays correspond with the numbers found in *The Complete Plays and Poems of William Shakespeare*, edited by W. A. Neilson and C. J. Hill, 1948.

I wish to thank my wife for typing the manuscript of this book and my colleagues, Professors Evelyn Scholl and Lawrence Babb, for reading it and offering helpful suggestions. Errors of fact or opinion remaining in the manual are entirely my own.

G. R. P.

A SHORT LIST OF CRITICAL WORKS

PROBABLY *the best single volume of criticism for the student to buy as a companion to his course is Mark Van Doren's* Shakespeare, *1953.*

Alexander, Peter. *Shakespeare's Life and Art*, 1939.

Bradley, A. C. *Shakespearean Tragedy*, 1904 (paperback, 1955).

Craig, Hardin. *An Interpretation of Shakespeare*, 1948.

Granville-Barker, Harley. *Prefaces to Shakespeare*, 1948.

Knight, G. Wilson. *The Wheel of Fire*, 1949; *The Imperial Theme*, 1951.

Spencer, Theodore. *Shakespeare and the Nature of Man*, 1942.

Tillyard, E. M. W. *Shakespeare's History Plays*, 1944; *Shakespeare's Problem Plays*, 1949; *Shakespeare's Last Plays*, 1938.

Traversi, D. A. *An Approach to Shakespeare*, 1954.

CONTENTS

1

Suggestions for Study

IN ENROLLING for a course in Shakespeare you well understood that you were going to be asked to read plays by the world's greatest dramatist. His works have had the extraordinary vitality to captivate theater audiences and readers for over three hundred and fifty years. That Shakespeare must have been a great showman you are quite willing to admit. But "showmanship," which itself is a quality challenging our analysis, is less important than Shakespeare's poetry, in the broadest sense. Shakespeare, the greatest poet in the English language, is a "maker" (to use the root of *poet*), of impressive human characters, moving stories of human fortune, and powerful utterance of passion. He is our greatest poet, then, not only in the intense expressiveness of his language, but in his handling of themes of human life. All of this creation he intended to be impersonated and spoken by actors before a living audience. As a man of the English Renaissance he wrote his interpretation of life for an audience who largely shared his social, religious, political, and literary ideas. It is certain that the most intensive study you have time for will only make a beginning of your understanding of Shakespeare. But in terms of the college course, you can achieve success by intensive study of the lines of the plays, as the indispensable first step toward critical judgment.

Further illumination of the meaning must come from the instructor and from reading criticism.

General suggestions

If the play is unfamiliar to you, and if time permits, read the drama through rapidly, without stopping to look at footnotes or to make any notations of your own. Then, perhaps according to class-assignments, go through the play intensively, scene by scene. Expect to derive an apt meaning from every line. If you get none, and if you are sure that you have looked up the sense of new or doubtful words in the glossarial notes and in a collegiate dictionary, then make a notation to ask the instructor for an interpretation in class. Here are several possible reasons why you may derive no meaning from a line: Some familiar word may have a sense unsuspected by you (see "Vocabulary," below); some philosophic or social idea may be implicit which you are ignorant of; or the line may have been garbled by Shakespeare, a scribe, or the printers (see "Text," below, Chapter 5).

Of course most instructors welcome sincere questions which reveal the students' difficulties; but if your teacher prefers to give an uninterrupted lecture, either consult him privately or do what scholarship demands, that is, investigate the diction of the obscure line in the *Oxford English Dictionary;* and consult the notes on the line which you will find in more fully edited texts of the play.[1]

For instance of an obscurity, in *Henry* IV, Part I, I. 3. 251-54, Hotspur cries out, concerning Bolingbroke:

Why, what a candy deal of courtesy

This fawning greyhound then did proffer me!

[1] George Lyman Kittredge annotates Shakespeare's diction very fully in his edition of the plays.

Look, "when his infant fortune came to age,"
And "gentle Harry Percy," and "kind cousin";
O, the devil take such cozeners!

Why does Hotspur interject *Look* before quoting
Bolingbroke? Are not the lines incoherent? As punctuated above, they are in fact incoherent; in this instance modern editors have not properly shown the
sense. The punctuation should be:

Why, what a candy deal of courtesy
This fawning greyhound then did proffer me
"Look when his infant fortune came to age"!
And "gentle Harry Percy," and "kind cousin";
O, the devil take such cozeners!

After we learn that *look when* is an obsolete idiom
meaning 'whenever,' the sense of the lines is perfectly
clear. The idiom was probably becoming obscure by
1623, when the editors of the First Folio put a period
after *me*, although even a comma was unnecessary.
Later editors also generally misunderstood and mis-
punctuated the lines.

At the end of each scene, pause to ask, What dramatic purpose has the scene served in the light of the
meaning of the whole play? Since Shakespeare soon
became a skillful playwright, most of his scenes will
be found to serve several purposes. However, this is
not always true. Occasionally he only wishes to mark
a lapse of time in the story or to provide an interval
while actors change costumes. But ordinarily, artistic
economy leads Shakespeare to use a necessary interlude for genuine dramatic meaning. For instance, the
Porter Scene in *Macbeth* allows Macbeth and his wife
to wash away the gore from their arms and change
costume; but Shakespeare has turned the irony of

the Porter's drunken soliloquy to great dramatic advantage.

In this connection never forget that the Shakespearean stage had no front curtain to drop at the end of the scene. As readers we receive a false impression from the decisiveness of our texts: "Exeunt. SCENE II. Enter . . ." We are likely to imagine a closing of the scene at this point. But in Shakespeare's theater a scene was ended just by the vacating of the stage by all the characters. The vacancy might be only for a moment; almost as one door closed behind the last man to leave the scene, another door opened to admit other characters. The smooth flow of scenes is to be remembered, then; and hence scenes are not to be thought of in isolation but in sequence, in context. Only this way can we estimate the dramatic quality of each upon the audience *in the theater*.

Character sketches

Because nineteenth century worshippers of Shakespeare laid too much emphasis on his success in character-drawing and neglected his other dramatic powers, contemporary criticism has recoiled to concentrate on imagery, metaphor, conventions, style, philosophic import, and other aspects. The correction was necessary. But it remains true that Shakespeare is the supreme master in truth and vividness of characterization, and that any young student who does not analyze the characters carefully is bound to go astray in critical opinion of the play.

A procedure that may prove helpful is to make sketches of the major characters while you are studying the play intensively. Assign a paragraph space in your notebook to each of the important persons, and as their traits are revealed in the successive scenes, jot down the traits as a single word, followed by a phrase naming the episode in which the trait is revealed. Thus, for Hotspur in *Henry* IV, Part I:

— fluency and eloquence of speech (excuse for not giving up prisoners to King's emissary on battle-field)
— tactlessness (same place)
— hot temper (after King orders him to produce the prisoners)
— love of wife (farewell to her, when leaving for Shrewsbury battle)
— vanity (cannot bear to hear Prince praised, conference of conspirators before battle).
And so on.

Such lists have at least two uses: They help you to clarify and correct your impressions of characters by drawing your attention to traits as they are gradually revealed; and they furnish excellent raw material for the inevitable examination questions that involve character-interpretation.

Summary of plot

This obvious device also has more value than the advantage of providing a form of review for examination. Probably no one attempts to summarize the action of a play after completing the reading of it, without finding that he has to look once again at certain episodes and speeches to ascertain the precise connection of motive or the manipulation of action by which one scene leads into another.

In addition, there may be a little more profit in making this summary after the completion of study of the play, for then you can better select those details which highlight the significance of the play, its central meaning, as well as those which, if omitted, may puzzle your memory at a later time.

Dramatic conventions

Both the theater and drama of Elizabethan times were descended from medieval forms, and naturally retained traditions of the medieval. But because the succeeding centuries have so much changed the theater, medieval conventions are foreign to us, and our ignorance of them leads to misconceptions about Shakespeare's intention and effect. It is impossible and unnecessary to attempt a survey of all such conventions here. Many of them will be defined in lectures and class discussion. But leading ones may be briefly noted here.

Many conventions were rooted in the morality plays of the late Middle Ages and early Renaissance. In the moralities, which were allegories, the persons are usually abstractions, like Meekness, Death, Patience, Lady Science, and Honest Recreation. Thus they represent one idea or quality and speak only within the narrow limits of that "character." They reveal their plans freely, for their single motivation must be understood clearly if the allegory is to achieve its meaning for the audience. In *Wyt and Science*, when Wit (intelligence) goes to woo Lady Science (learning), and refuses the help of Instruction, the giant Tediousness enters the stage with a visor over his face and a club in his hand: "Oh, the body of me! What beasts are those that don't try to flee from Tediousness's nose, but instead, rouse me out of my nest when I should be at ease to rest me! That Wit, that villain, that wretch, a shame take him — surely it is he that makes himself so bold as, without my permission, to stalk by my door, to find that whore, Science, and wed her! But I despise her and before I let Wit come nigh her, the knave's head shall ache. . . . This mall shall beat him to dust." Thus the character explains himself and forecasts the action.

Self-revelation carries over into the Elizabethan drama. It is found, obviously, in asides and in soliloquies; and the student should remember that because soliloquies set forth the character's own conception of his motives they demand very careful study. (Some students make a list of major soliloquies in the play, for review.) A dramatic character uses no conscious concealment in soliloquy. A parallel to Tediousness's speech quoted above may be seen in Prince Hal's famous soliloquy in *Henry* IV, Part I, I. 2. 218-240. Viewed in the light of medieval tradition, Hal sets forth his present motives and even his future reformation, but without the priggishness we are inclined to read into the speech.

The dramatic advantage of self-revelation is its economy. With the minimum of lines and time, the dramatic relation of the character is set in the minds of the audience. The play can then move on to development of the situation. Though we are accustomed by both fiction and modern drama to a slower, "realistic" process of revelation of character, we need not assume that the older method is less artistic. It will be wiser for us to reconsider the essential purposes of dramatic art and evaluate all the means that may be chosen to accomplish the purposes. But that subject is not to be dealt with here.

Sometimes characters in Shakespearean drama seem like personifications of one particular quality. The tendency is less noticeable in Shakespeare's own plays than in those of his contemporaries, for Shakespeare's grasp of human nature was so complete that even minor characters seem to have human depth. However, the influence of the morality tradition may be found in John of Gaunt, the personification of patriotism in *Richard* II. (But Gaunt is also saddened fatherhood and affronted wisdom.) Angelo of *Measure for Measure* might have played a part in a morality, and have been named *Pride of Virtue*. A special feature of late morality drama was the comic figure of the Vice, an aide of the devil, who became general mischief-maker and included even his master among his victims. But he was always carried off at last to Hell on the devil's back. Modern scholars have attempted to trace the basic elements of the Vice in such different persons as Falstaff (*Henry* iv), Edmund (*King Lear*), and Iago (*Othello*).

Edmund's death-bed conversion from evil-doing to repentance (*King Lear*), Duke Frederick the Usurper's unexpected renunciation of the world (*As You Like It*), and Leontes's instantaneous recovery from evil passion (*The Winter's Tale*) remind us of the sudden heartfelt repentance that Mankind and Everyman show when Death confronts them in the moralities. However, abrupt conversions from evil to good are more striking in the plays of dramatists other than Shakespeare.

From both moralities and miracle plays came the tradition of combining broad comedy with serious drama. For many years no fact about Elizabethan drama was a more familiar bone for the critics to contend over than Shakespeare's mingling of comic scenes in his tragedies. Doubtless the English audience had been trained by hundreds of years of experience to look for the "clowns" and their farce, no matter what the play. And as a practical necessity, an acting company must have had to keep a successful comedian on their roster. For him a part must be provided even in serious plays. For him was created Peter, in *Romeo and Juliet*; the court fools in *As You Like It, Twelfth Night, King Lear*, and other plays; the Drunken Porter in *Macbeth*; the Clown in *Othello*; and the Countryman in *Antony and Cleopatra*.

Finally, from the medieval stages came the tradition of easy, imaginary changes of scene. Characters in medieval and Elizabethan dramas passed rapidly from one imagined locality to another, simply by moving about the stage. Medieval staging was "multiple," the various areas on the platform being used for specific places, or "houses," for instance, the house of God, that of the devil, and those of other characters like Flesh, the World and Covetousness. There was also a general, or unlocalized, playing area, the *platea*. This method of staging was transferred to the popular theaters of Queen Elizabeth's reign. The platform stage (see "Shakespeare's Theater," Chapter 2) was usually an unlocalized area; but when, occasionally, a particular locality had to be employed in the action, it was likely to be represented by a door in the rear wall of the stage, or a balcony above, or by the low platform, used as a dais for the royal throne and also as a hill-top or other elevation. The inner stage (or perhaps a curtain-covered "house" in front of the stage-wall) served for a study, a bedroom, a tent, or a cell. Carrying a table on to the outer stage localized it as a Senate chamber or a banquet hall; pushing out a bed made it a bedroom; enthroning the king on his "state" (large chair) made it a hall of state. Movement of the characters about the stage could change the setting, for instance, from an army camp to the space before walls of a castle or a city.

Perhaps the chief things for the student to remember are that these shifts of locale are easy and rapid. Furthermore, a great many scenes are not localized at all, and do not need to be. The excitement and significance of the action are what count, not the place. Modern editions of Shakespeare emphasize too much the particular localities of the scenes.

Three other dramatic conventions not definitely connected with medieval drama may be mentioned briefly. One concerns the sudden onsets of destructive passion which affect the lives of a number of Shakespeare's heroes. Today we are accustomed by the art of prose fiction to a gradual development of character and passion, a method which we think "realistic." But Shakespeare knew that his audience were used to a compact representation of experience, and that they readily accepted rapid psychological changes in stage-characters, in order that the play might pass on swiftly to its great climaxes. Consequently, we sometimes think

Shakespeare's preparation for a tragic emotion is very slight. Passion overwhelms its victims like a hurricane. King Lear, Leontes (in *A Winter's Tale*), and Othello are examples of this convention. However, for us to make a critical evaluation of such dramatic situations is not easy, for the dramatist did not absolve his hero from responsibility for his acts performed under the sway of wrath or jealousy. Ancient conceptions of human physiology and psychology and Stoic philosophy furnish part of the background of ideas for portraying "passion's slaves"; but the Christian doctrines of free will, sin, punishment, and grace are equally important. As a result, human action becomes decidedly complex, even mysterious. No simple formula makes a satisfactory interpretation of the hero's behavior.

Second, Shakespeare at times seems to use one of his characters for a dramatic purpose not clearly consistent with the traits of that character as they have been set for us earlier. One critic has called this "depersonalization." [2] A famous example is Enobarbus' admiring description of Cleopatra, a woman whom he despises, in *Antony and Cleopatra*, II. 2. 195-245. Shakespeare's problem seems to be that he wishes a dramatic note to be sounded at this point, but has no appropriate character to utter it. He wishes Cleopatra's allure, which has been absent from the stage for several scenes, to be felt, ironically, at the moment when Antony appears to have regained his independence by the pact with Caesar and Octavia. (We see Cleopatra's power further symbolized in the next scene when the Soothsayer confirms Antony's intention to return to Alexandria.) Another example, perhaps less easy to justify, is Mercutio's Queen Mab speech in *Romeo and Juliet*, I. 4. 53-94. In objecting to these passages the scholar in his study has probably been too much concerned with consistency of character and

[2] S. L. Bethell, *Shakespeare and the Popular Dramatic Tradition*, 107-116.

too little with dramatic effects upon the audience's imagination. Certainly the Elizabethan audience's relish for imaginative language partly justifies Shakespeare.

Finally, Shakespeare occasionally uses two schemes of time within a series of scenes, the span of one time-scheme being longer than that of the other. In *King Lear*, for instance, two plots, that of Lear and his daughters and that of Gloucester and his sons, begin within a period of twenty-four hours' time. Lear abandons Cordelia and goes to live with Goneril. A few hours later (I. 2. 23-24) Edmund has poisoned Gloucester's mind against his brother Edgar and promises to demonstrate Edgar's malice "this very evening." About two weeks later (I. 3 and 4) Lear discovers Goneril's hatred of him. That same night (II. 1. 5) by a trick Edmund demonstrates Edgar's villainy to Gloucester. Thus we see what has been called "long" and "short" time utilized alternately. The student should note that the two time schemes are not maintained separately throughout the entire play, but fuse later on. The need for separate time orders is only incidental and temporary. Shakespeare avoids drawing attention to it quite skillfully, as one can see by examining the time references in the scenes of *Lear* cited above. Each plot obeys its own necessities of time, but above all, Shakespeare wishes to counterpoint the themes of two plots, to intensify emotion and meaning. He successfully relies on dramatic intensity to exclude from the audience's awareness the incongruities of time.

Vocabulary

Shakespeare wrote and spoke Early Modern English. In grammar, pronunciation, and significance, his language is substantially our own. Yet there are some differences — chiefly those in the senses of words — which mislead or frustrate the modern student. Consequently, college texts of Shakespeare are usually equipped with a vocabulary, or glossary, more or less full. Probably no modern edition relegates the glossary to the end of the volume, for it is too inconvenient in that position. Even to have to drop one's eyes to the foot of the page is troublesome enough; but on the usual double-column page the notes must go at the foot, for there is no room in the margins. Rarely are the vocabulary notes complete enough to satisfy the instructor. But to make them fuller would be to make the "complete works" in one volume too bulky to be carried. Something must be sacrificed.

The linguistic difficulties that face the student may be partly solved if he will remember that the differences between Shakespeare's vocabulary and our own are principally of two kinds: 1] Shakespeare's use of words that are now obsolete. We ordinarily recognize the strangeness of these at once, and also know our duty of looking them up in the glossary or a dictionary. The verb to *tarre* and the noun *cinquepace* are examples. 2] Shakespeare's use of words which are identical in form with familiar words of today, but which had a different meaning in Shakespeare's time. Obviously, the difficulty with these is that we are not aware of the difference and so read into the lines a sense quite different from that which the poet intended. For instance, *Stand close!* in Shakespeare means 'Stand hidden,' that is, "Withdraw into hiding." (The Latin sense of *clausus* is retained in Elizabethan English.)

In attacking the first problem of Shakespeare's vocabulary, some students have used the following device: Before studying a scene they run through the glossarial notes and put a dot under every word in the lines of the play for which a note is provided at the foot of the page. Thus they know when to look down.

In solving the problem of the second difficulty mentioned above, it is some comfort to be told that the number of *oft-repeated words which look like ours but have a different sense* is relatively small. In fact, it is possible to memorize many or all of them in a semester's study and thus make one's reading of the plays faster and more authoritative with comparatively small trouble. You are therefore invited to *memorize* the following list, in reasonable doses. This list of terms is certainly not complete; and you may wish to add to it many words of less frequency, such as *thought* in the sense of 'melancholy.' You will also have a great advantage if you have studied Latin and will recall the Latin sense as meant by Shakespeare, instead of the modern one — for instance, *curious* in the sense 'careful,' 'accurate.' Editors occasionally gloss these words in their notes to the plays; but precisely because the words recur so often, they cannot be noted regularly. Hence the value of a purposeful effort on your part. It is important to add that the meanings listed here are not the only ones that may be found in Shakespeare. But they are the common ones.

Finally, you will be surprised to find how often a desk or collegiate dictionary will be useful to you in studying the plays.

abuse (v), to deceive.
addition, a man's title.
admire, wonder at.
affect, to love passionately.
affection, passionate love.
annoy, harm.
aye (adv.), ever.
banquet, dessert of sweetmeats, fruit and wine.
blood, lust or anger.
brave, excellent, splendid.
close (adj.), concealed.
companion, rascal, base fellow.
conceit, a concept, a clever idea.
conceive, to understand.

confusion, utter ruin.
convince, overcome, conquer.
cousin, coz, any relative beyond parent, child, or sibling.
curst, shrewish, vicious.
dear, hard, grievous (in addition to our meanings).
doubt, suspicion.
fancy (n.), love, passion.
fantasy, imagination or fancy.
favor (n.), features, "looks."
folly, lust.
fond, foolish.

foul, ugly.

gentle, noble, aristocratic.

go, walk.

home (adv.), to the center of the target, deep.

honest, (of a woman) chaste; (of a man) candid, honorable.

idle, useless, unprofitable.

jealous, suspicious.

kind (n.), the nature of the species (e.g., of the dog or the man).

let, hinder.

look how, however. (Other indefinite relative pronouns and adverbs are similarly formed: *look who, look when, look where.*)

mere, entire, perfect.

methinks, it appears to me (*not* 'I think').

naught, evil.

naughty, evil.

nice, fastidious.

practice, plot.

prevent, arrive before another.

proper, handsome.

quick, alive.

quicken, to make alive.

sad, serious, heavy (*not* mournful).

shrewd, sharp, scolding.

speed, thrive, prosper.

still, always.

tall, brave, skillful.

2

Shakespeare's Theater and Company

The Theater

In Shakespeare's day London was largely a city
of wooden structures, as it had been in the Middle Ages.
It is not surprising, therefore, that the theaters were
built of wood, and that in course of time they have all
disappeared by having been dismantled or burned down.
Indeed, only one drawing of the interior of an Elizabethan theater has survived from Shakespeare's lifetime, the DeWitt sketch of the Swan theater; but we
have several engravings which show, with some disagreement about details, the exterior of a number of
playhouses. The drawing of the Swan, the specifica-
tions for the construction of the Fortune theater which
have been preserved, and the action of the plays themselves furnish students of the drama with most of their
data and their theories about the interior of Shakespeare's theater, the Globe.

Doubtless the leading fact about the Elizabethan
public theaters, of which the Globe was the most
famous, is the prominence of the platform stage. The
platform stage was basic to the structure of the theater
and to dramatic effects. We are not likely to forget
this importance if we understand that in the earliest
English theaters, as in the inn-yards which preceded
them as places for acting, the players set up a scaffold

of boards on trestles or "horses"; on one end of it was a curtained booth or dressing room. The audience stood around at least three-fourths of this platform. Although it was about head-high, they were prevented from seeing underneath the stage by a cloth draped around the scaffold from the stage floor to the ground. This concealment allowed for a sub-stage, the region of underground or Hell.

This basic structure was transferred to permanent theater buildings with very little change. The five-and-a-half-foot height was retained as well as the drapes (replaced in one theater by wooden paneling) for concealment. The platform was approximately forty feet wide and twenty-eight feet in depth from its front to the rear wall of the stage. One or two trapdoors were constructed in the floor of the stage. Through a trap an actor could rise from Hell into the sunlight; or through the drapes he could emerge into the space beside the platform.

Probably the chief development of the primitive theater was the elaboration of the stage wall, the wall of the dressing room or tiring house (i.e., attiring house) at the back of the stage. The DeWitt drawing shows two double doors leading into this tiring room; but many modern scholars believe that the area backstage had been converted into a rectangular "study," or inner stage,[1] perhaps ten feet in depth and ten to twenty feet wide — and provided with a draw curtain at the front. The arrangements of the inner stage and even its existence are disputed, for they are based on inference from stage directions. That there was a "study," at times used for a tomb, a prison cell, a bedroom, or a shop, is perfectly sure; but it may have been a curtained booth set *in front* of a tiring room wall and with access from behind through a tiring room door.

---

[1] *Inner stage* is a modern term in common use.

More certain is the "upper stage," or "lord's room," a second-floor playing space above the tiring room or inner stage. The upper stage was actually a continuation of a gallery which ran around the interior of the auditorium. Though certainly used in about half of Shakespeare's plays for brief scenes introduced by stage directions like *Enter on the walls, Enter aloft, Enter above*, it is probable that the usefulness of this area was limited by the presence of spectators who were allowed to occupy seats in it, and who may have had to squeeze together to permit the passing of the actors. But such close contact with the actors offered no shock to these gentlemen, for the whole theater provided an almost equal intimacy with the stage. Some scholars have theorized about a third level, the "music room," which is not revealed in the DeWitt drawing, but may not be incongruous with it. If the room was located above the upper stage, it could have served as the source of music off-stage.

Certainly, from above either the second- or the third-level upper stage a roof projected over about one-third of the platform, to give the actors some protection from direct sun and rain and, perhaps more importantly, to furnish a place from which celestial persons like gods and angels might be lowered. This roof was called "the heavens"; it was large enough from top to bottom to permit actors to enter it and be lowered through trapdoors. Above the heavens was a "hut" from which a cannon charged with powder and wadding simulated battle noises and flashes of lightning. At the same time cannonballs, dropping from trough to trough, roared like thunder.

The rear wall of the stage, where not broken by doors or possibly by the curtain of the inner stage, was probably carved and painted with mythological or historical figures. Somewhere along its surface (or over one of its doors) hung the arras, a tapestry behind which a character could conceal himself. Whatever the precise decoration of the stage walls, two things we are sure of — that there was no scenery in the modern sense and no change of the backdrop or decor during a play. The dialogue and the action revealed the place, if the audience needed to know the place. Many scenes in Shakespeare's drama are "unlocalized"; that is, no place needs to be present in the audience's consciousness, and therefore no place is mentioned.

So far we have concentrated upon the heart of the theater, the stage and its accouterments. The remainder of the building offered less that is unfamiliar to modern playgoers. Immediately surrounding the stage was a large, unfloored space, open to the sky and called "the pit," where most of the audience stood

The Globe Theater as Reconstructed by Richard Southern. (*From Shakespeare Survey*, xii (1959), *Plate* ii, *by permission of the Cambridge University Press, publishers.*)

for the two or two and a half hours' time of the play. Naturally, these people were called "the groundlings" and sometimes, because of their lower-class fondness for much garlic, "the stinkards." Surrounding the pit and attached to the walls of the building were two or three galleries, one above the other, in which were benches or chairs. These galleries were roofed over. The roof of the topmost gallery was, of course, also the roof of the theater; at the Globe it was of thatch.

All the spectators seem to have entered the building through one large door opposite the stage. Having paid their admission (approximately twenty-five cents in today's value) to the "gatherer," they stationed themselves in the pit or paid another fee for the comfort and seclusion of the gallery. If Ben Jonson spoke accurately in his Induction to *Bartholomew Fair*, played in 1614, the admission to the Hope Theater cost sixpence; desirable places in the galleries cost a shilling, eighteenpence, two shillings, or a half a crown. Perhaps the half-crown gentlemen sat on stools in the lord's room or on the stage itself:

> When yong *Rogero* goes to see a play,
>
> His pleasure is you place him on the Stage,
>
> The better to demonstrate his aray,
>
> And how he sits attended by his Page,
>
> That onely serves to fill those pipes with smoke,
>
> For which he pawned hath his riding Cloke.[2]

Those who stood in the pit were probably apprentices, seventeen to twenty-four years old; artisans and tradesmen; professional "gallants," fellows who dressed like gentlemen and wore a sword, but lived by gambling, "cozening" (swindling), or other sharp practices; and farmers and other country-folk visiting the city. Those who occupied the galleries must have been the well-to-

[2] Henry Parrot, *Laquei Ridiculosi*, 1613, signature [C6v].

do: gentlemen and lords, students at the Inns of Court (colleges of law), successful tradesmen, sons of country gentry playing the man-about-town in London. In all parts of the auditorium women were found, the respectable as well as the disreputable. In the opinion of Professor Alfred Harbage, Shakespeare's audience was not a "selected" one, though youth predominated over age, male over female, the worldly over the pious.[3]

In number the average audience may have been about 1250; three or four of the theaters had a capacity between 2000 and 3000. In good years, when epidemics of plague or other mischances did not shorten the season, actors played almost daily to large audiences for nine or ten months. The auditors seem to have been enthusiastic, but not uproarious or much noisier than a modern movie audience in a college town. Some of them smoked, drank bottle ale, munched nuts and apples, laughed loudly, and hissed the things they did not like. But no doubt a large number behaved more decorously. The literary style of the plays indicates that the audience were good listeners to poetry and rhetoric. When Ben Jonson lectures them, it is not for noise or inattention, but for lack of understanding.

The Company

The companies of actors in Shakespeare's England are best understood through an elementary knowledge of the origin of the acting profession.

The early Middle Ages had no professional actors and no theaters designed especially for drama. The professional entertainers of that time were minstrels, acrobats, jugglers, conjurors, and owners of trained animals. These performers often traveled in troupes, probably under the leadership of the minstrel, the cleverest of the team, a reciter of gestes or romances. By the fourteenth century, if not earlier, many troupes

[3] *Shakespeare's Audience,* 1941, p. 90.

had come to be employed in the households of great lords. At festival times they furnished vaudeville shows for the amusement of the lord and his guests. At other seasons they took to the road and performed in towns and villages.

Meantime, in the liturgical worship of the Catholic Church a primitive drama had begun to develop. Having originated as simple, short dialogues in the service of Matins at Easter, Christmas, and other festivals, religious drama grew and flourished under the favor of the Church, which saw in it an effective means of instructing the people in the whole Biblical story of God's dealings with men. As it expanded greatly, religious drama had to be removed from the liturgical service and to begin its independent existence, which has proved to be the source of our own drama. Because of the crowds it attracted, it also had to be moved out of the church building, first into the church-yard, thence to the squares of the town. Yet in purpose it continued to be essentially the same, although by the fifteenth century the preparation of the pageants, i.e., movable stages, was entrusted to laymen of the trade guilds, such as the merchants, the carpenters, and the tilers. However, we are chiefly concerned here with the actors of the plays. They, like the dramatists, were mostly "clerks," that is, clerics, men in Holy Orders. (Comparatively few other people were literate enough to compose plays or study parts.) If laymen sometimes had minor roles, clerics usually had the major ones. In any case, all were amateurs. But the word does not imply crudity of performance. For these Miracle plays, which often reach a level of excellence that the modern world is only beginning to appreciate, demanded con-siderable skill of the actors.

In course of time this flourishing religious drama affected private social entertainment and consequently the professional troupes led by the minstrels. At least as early as the fifteenth century there are records of plays produced in the great houses of nobility during seasons of festivity. The actors might be boys from a neighboring cathedral school or choir, or they might be adult men, minstrels, musicians, tutors of the lord's children. At the royal court and in the homes of the greatest nobility dramatic productions came to be frequent forms of entertainment, and the players are mentioned in account books, at first as "minstrels," later as "players" or "actors." At Selby Abbey in 1398 the Duke of Northumberland's four *minstrels* performed; at the same place in 1479 the Duke of Gloucester's *actors* played.[4]

Clearly, the next step had been taken: The lord had added this group of actors to his corps of servants and had given them (if they had had no position in his household) an official status. On special occasions they wore the lord's livery, or servants' uniform, and marched in wedding or funeral processions or at coronations. They were expected to provide an Interlude or Morality play for celebrations. Sometimes the lord's chaplain was also their playwright.

No doubt the causes which combined to produce a class of professional actors in England were complex. But surely an important cause is the development of the Interlude. As a dramatic genre the Interlude ranges through a great variety, from moral allegory to satiric farce. Though it had no fixed form or purpose, its common position as part of the entertainment in the evening, following dinner in the great hall of the castle, tended to enhance its comic quality. However, we are mainly interested here in the fact that the lord's troupe of entertainers might join with the chaplain and the choir boys to make a cast for playing the Interlude. Doubtless it was in this way that minstrels, musicians, jesters, and other entertainers were led to the occupation of acting.

[4] Glynne Wickham, *Early English Stages 1300 to 1660*, vol. I (1959), 267.

The Interlude was much involved with the educational and social, as well as the religious, developments of the Renaissance, at the end of the fifteenth and beginning of the sixteenth centuries. Not only did a new interpretation of classical literature enter England from the Continent, but new accomplishments were being expected of a gentleman. No longer could the aristocracy leave learning and literature entirely to the clergy; now a nobleman was expected to be able to read, to own books, to know something of the Roman poets, including the dramatists. Though Cardinal John Morton himself was not by birth an aristocrat, yet it was for Morton's aristocratic guests that his chaplain, Henry Medwall, wrote the lively Interlude *Fulgens and Lucrece*, probably performed at Christmas in 1497. The theme is borrowed from a *controversia*, or debate, written by an Italian, who, in turn, imitated Cicero. It is possible that *Fulgens and Lucrece* was acted chiefly by professionals who, if the play seemed fit for the populace, could have added it to their repertory for performance in innyards or at fairs.

For records prove that the troupes of actors continued the practice of traveling about the country as their predecessors, the minstrels, had done. At the same time they kept their allegiance to their patron-lord and were obligated to give performances at festivities in his house. This arrangement favored the lord, who did not wish to pay a company of actors, many of whom would necessarily be idle in his household for days or weeks together; it favored the actors, for they developed their skill and, with luck, made a better income. And above all, they were protected from the law. The law of England was severe on vagabonds and masterless men. If considered dangerous rogues, they were branded with R on the left shoulder and sent to their home parishes (and to the jobs they had presumably abandoned); if convicted the second time, they were felons and could be hanged. Traveling acrobats, jugglers, and actors all came under the statute against vagabonds.[5] But actors who could prove their legal service of a lord were not vagabonds.

This short history explains several things about the profession of acting in sixteenth century England. For one, all actors were men or boys, the boys being assigned the parts of women. The exclusion of women from an active part in the Church's liturgy partly explains the traditional exclusion of women from acting. Like the Church Fathers, modern divines would have been scandalized at the idea of women on the stage. The shifting personnel and wandering life of the early companies would not favor, though it did not absolutely forbid, the presence of women. Second, we now see why the companies always bear the name of a nobleman or a monarch — the Lord Strange's Men, the Earl of Worcester's Men, the Queen's Men — instead of the name of a manager or a theater. It is true, of course, that there were also companies exclusively of boy actors, who were ostensibly choir boys of one or other of the important chapels in London. The indirect influence of the boy-companies on Shakespeare's drama will be mentioned again, below. Finally, the adult actor's legal position among riff-raff, his transparent evasion of the law against roguery, was a social stigma against which the profession had to struggle until generations later. When Shakespeare became an actor, he must have deeply grieved the heart of his father and mother, and he surely gave himself cause for extreme discomfort at times. In one of his sonnets he speaks ruefully of the stain of his profession clinging to him like that on a dyer's hand. But in his own lifetime the social status of actors improved.

As is noted in Chapter 4, the sketch of Shakespeare's life, we have no evidence as to which company Shakespeare joined on first coming to London, nor, in fact,

[5] Sir Edmund Coke, *The Third Part of the Institutes,* 1660, Cap. xi, signature P₂r.

as to the year when he first came. If he entered the theatrical world between 1588 and 1591, he possibly began with one of three companies, the Lord Strange's, the Lord Admiral's, or the Earl of Pembroke's. All companies seem to have experienced hard times during this period, and Strange's and the Admiral's may have merged in order to survive; but they separated again around 1594. Whether Shakespeare was with them or Pembroke's is uncertain. However, by the summer of 1594 the group formerly known as Lord Strange's Men had obtained the patronage of Henry Lord Hunsdon, Lord Chamberlain to the Queen, and Shakespeare was with them, for in 1595 he had become even a shareholder. Thenceforth for most of the time till the death of the Queen in 1603 the company kept the title, "The Lord Chamberlain's Men." Then their merits were recognized by James I himself, and they became Grooms of the Chamber in Ordinary, and were styled the King's Men until the final dissolution of the theaters in 1642. Their pre-eminence over their chief rivals, the Lord Admiral's Men (afterwards, 1603-1612, Prince Henry's Men), was unmistakable by 1603 and was never questioned in Stuart times.

It should be noted that a permanent nucleus of several shrewd and gifted men carried this company to success and to enjoyment of profits as shareholders. The shareholders probably numbered from nine to twelve men at different times; those of longest continuance were Henry Condell, John Heminge, Shakespeare, Richard Burbage, William Sly, and Augustine Philips. Their greatest tragedian was Burbage. Inevitably he was compared with Ned Alleyn, the master tragedian of the Admiral's Men, player of Marlowe's heroes, such as Dr. Faustus and Tamburlaine. Today Burbage is commonly supposed the greater, but there was probably little to choose between them. For Burbage were written the roles of Hamlet, Othello, Lear, and Macbeth; to some degree, then, we owe it to the genius of this great actor that Shakespeare wrote the magnificent poetry of these roles. "Stuttering Heminges" played old men's parts and is said also to have been the first Falstaff. A more famous comedian was Will Kempe, member of the company until 1599, when he fell into disagreement with his mates (he was then a shareholder) and withdrew.

When the company were given a new patent and new patronage, as the King's Company, in 1603, the six men first named above were listed, plus three more. One of the new ones, Robert Armin, had become Kempe's successor as the leading comedian; for him were written the parts of the court fools in *Twelfth Night* and *King Lear*. We can infer the differences between Will Kempe's and Robert Armin's styles of comic acting not only from anecdotes about them, but also from comparison of the parts of Bottom (*A Midsummer Night's Dream*) and Launcelot Gobbo (*The Merchant of Venice*) with the court fools of the later plays. Kempe seems to have won favor in roles in which he impersonated a bumptious, impudent, seemingly stupid fellow with a streak of cunning in him. He probably grimaced, used much business, and sometimes adlibbed to the audience. He certainly could dance energetically, for in 1600 he jigged all the way to Norwich to win a bet. His voice was perhaps not very tuneful, for songs are not numerous in the parts that we suppose he played; yet he was widely known as a master of the song and dance called the "jig," which was a vaudeville act that followed the performance of a play. Kempe was a strong asset to his company. Not a gentleman in London, it is said in a play of about 1600, or "a country wench that can dance Sellenger's Round, but can talk of Dick Burbage and Will Kempe."

It is usual to say that Armin was a subtler comedian, a more genuinely witty fellow who adapted himself better to tones of irony in a play. It is possible that some critics have exaggerated the differences by forgetting the broad parts that Shakespeare wrote for Armin in *Othello, Troilus and Cressida, Measure for Measure,* and *Antony and Cleopatra.* However, it seems undeniable that he was a better singer than Kempe, and that he was capable of giving to his role of jester an element of pathos or wry humor that is lacking in the parts of Bottom and Peter (in *Romeo and Juliet*), which were Kempe's. Whereas the audience seem to have laughed at Kempe's crude blunders with words and his broad puns and bawdy talk, they probably enjoyed Armin's finesse and sharpness in word-play. Yet the part of Touchstone in *As You Like It* presents a difficulty. The probable date of the play, 1599, gives no help in deciding for which comedian Touchstone was written. It is a witty enough role for Armin; but the songs in the play are sung by other characters, except for two small scraps that sound like parody.

What parts did Shakespeare himself play? and how well did he play them? About 1610 a minor poet named John Davies of Hereford wrote in an epigram that Shakespeare played "Kingly parts in sport." The last phrase, in its context, may mean only "as an actor." At the beginning of the eighteenth century Nicholas Rowe mentioned a stage tradition that the dramatist played the Ghost in *Hamlet*; at the end of that century another tradition records that he acted old Adam in *As You Like It.* These unverified reports are disappointing and suggest a mediocre ability. Yet John Aubrey, the biographer, writing sixty or seventy years after Shakespeare's death, said he had learned that Shakespeare "did act exceedingly well"; and in 1592, near the beginning of the poet's career, a rival playwright, Henry Chettle, politely described him as "exelent in the qualitie he professes," i.e., acting. Jonson listed Shakespeare first among the ten "principal comedians" of *Every Man in His Humour* and also named him among the eight "principal tragedians" of *Sejanus.* Both these lists appeared in the *Works* of

1616, after Shakespeare had retired from the theater (possibly even after his death) ; they are unquestionably true in their essential point, but they do not reveal which part Shakespeare took in either play. However, an absolutely safe inference from these slight bits of evidence is that Shakespeare was competent enough as actor to play at least a minor role along with Burbage, John Lowin, and other masters in a difficult classical tragedy at a time when his demonstrated value to his company was chiefly in the composition of successful plays. For *Sejanus* was produced in 1603, nine years at least after Shakespeare had joined the company.

The companies of boy-actors have been mentioned above ; something may be said here about their relation to the King's Men and to Shakespeare. Though other juvenile companies acted from time to time, two troupes stand out in dramatic history as rivals to each other and to the adult actors : The Children of the Chapel Royal, playing in an indoor theater in the Blackfriars district, and hence called the Blackfriars Boys ; and the Children of St. Paul's Chapel, playing in a similar hall somewhere near the Cathedral of London, and called the Paul's Boys. In origin both companies were boy-choirs, intelligent youngsters with fine voices. Their musical training, and performances, however, did not occupy all their time ; and their ambitious trainers devoted part of the surplus to producing plays. Financial backing was soon found for what was in truth professional theater. These two companies flourished especially from about 1599 to 1606, a period indeed of extraordinary dramatic activity in London and a time when the adult-companies could have dispensed, as they thought, with this extra competition.

American students may wonder how the Elizabethan audience could believe juvenile actors to be of almost equal merit with adults. The reasons are not really obscure. First, the boys had some years of training, and there is no doubt that many of them became very adept

— in fact, as Hamlet points out, many of them were so excellent that they remained actors when they grew up. Secondly, playwrights tended to adapt their works for the boys' limitations and abilities. In particular, the boy companies featured comedy (though, of course, tragedies were also written for them) ; and usually their plays contained a good deal of music, especially songs. The comedies were spiced with satire and topical allusion; in fact, the managers of these troupes were more often in trouble with the government and the Church than were the adult companies, precisely because of their bold satires which were certainly introduced to create talk in the town and enlarge the audience. Furthermore, the boys played throughout the winter, when the monarch and the courtiers were all in London; and they played indoors, in smaller auditoriums and in the evening by candlelight. (In contrast, of course, the audience at the Globe watched a performance under the open sky, which was often grey in the winter and likely to rain on the groundlings ; and the afternoon hours of performance conflicted with other daytime activities, at least with the stroll through Paul's Walk — the main aisle of St. Paul's cathedral, a place of meetings.) Finally, the admission at the private theaters was higher, and the audience was therefore more fashionable.

The best known allusion to the rivalry of the boy companies with the adult ones is the discussion of them in *Hamlet* (II. 2. 341-379) ; and it makes clear that the King's Men felt the pinch which resulted from the loss of part of their audience. However, is the activity of the boys' companies really discernible in any important way in Shakespeare's dramas? An immediate effect can hardly be distinguished in his major dramas ; but in some lesser plays assignable to the period 1599-1606 scholars have found Shakespeare's attempt to accommodate to the vogue of satire, the specialty of the boys. *Troilus and Cressida* is the most notable example; though probably written for performance at one of the

Inns of Court, it could as well have been presented at a private theater, and in fact law students from the Inns comprised a considerable part of the audience at the private theaters. *Troilus and Cressida* presents an ancient love-story used as a medium of satire against the heroic romance of the Troy-legend and against war in general. *Measure for Measure* also has subordinate actions and characters which probably owe much to the pungent realism of Middleton's and Marston's satiric comedies, *ca.* 1604-1608. With less assurance, one may perceive the influence of the vogue of satire in parts of *All's Well That Ends Well* and in the very theme of *Timon of Athens,* as well as its expression.

Although the boy companies became less strongly competitive with the adults after 1606, the King's Men had come to recognize a significant change in theater business. They decided to cater more effectively to the special audience of the private theaters. They acquired the lease of the Blackfriars Theater in 1608 and after that year began to occupy it during the winter seasons. They did not, of course, give up the Globe Theater; in fact, after it burned in 1613, they rebuilt it. But by means of the two theaters they took full advantage of the established taste for sophistication in drama and of the smaller, elite audience. About the time of Shakespeare's retirement from the theater, they adopted John Fletcher as their dramatist par excellence, a writer whose comedies and tragicomedies were keyed exactly for the Blackfriars audience.

It is likely that Shakespeare, when he wrote for the Blackfriars, as he surely did on occasion, adapted his tragicomedies, or "romances," to fit that audience's taste. This modification has to be inferred from the qualities of the plays themselves, not from external evidence; for the only surviving records of original performances tell us that *The Winter's Tale* and *Cymbeline* were staged at the Globe, and that *The Winter's Tale* and *The Tempest* were twice presented at Court. However, absence of records from the Blackfriars of course does not forbid us to believe that these plays were also presented there. Probably the best view of Shakespeare's accomplishment is expressed by saying that from long experience he aimed to satisfy both audiences and that he succeeded.

3

Some Elizabethan Attitudes Reflected in Drama

LIKE PEOPLE today Elizabethan Englishmen spoke often of the disturbing changes they saw in their world. Yet, although in some respects their attitudes were beginning to differ sharply from those of the past, in most matters we find their conventions clearly related to those of the Middle Ages.

Marriage and women's place in society

Let us begin with customs related to courtship and marriage. Among all classes except the poorest, a marriageable girl was expected to possess a dowry, that is, money, real estate, or other property, with which to benefit her husband. Quite reasonably, the wealthier the girl's father was, the larger the dowry the husband could expect to receive. Hence, among well-to-do merchants and financiers, as well as among the gentry, the material aspect of marriage often assumed greater importance than the love of the man and woman or their fitness for each other in general.[1] The most chivalrous

[1] Speaking of the Middle Ages, C. S. Lewis says: "Marriages had nothing to do with love, and no 'nonsense' about marriage was tolerated. All matches were matches of interest . . ." *The Allegory of Love,* 1958, p. 13. Though Lewis has in mind only the aristocracy, and though exceptions can always be found, the generalization is probably as true for the Renaissance period as for the medieval.

Elizabethan courtier, Sir Philip Sidney, married, not the girl he had fallen in love with, but a wealthy heiress; and the philosopher Sir Francis Bacon at forty-five married the daughter of a prosperous alderman of London to help him pay his debts. Of course mere money or real estate did not always replace love as a motive to marriage; the poet John Donne married for love. But in general those who "married well" married to their material advantage.

This custom throws light on certain incidents in Shakespeare's plays. When Petruchio, in *The Taming of the Shrew*, says

> As wealth is burden of my wooing dance . . .
>
> I come to wive it wealthily in Padua;
>
> If wealthily, then happily, in Padua
>
> (I. 2. 68, 75-76.)

the audience think no worse of him for materialism; if anything, they like him the better for his candor. On the other hand, when King Lear in anger withdraws all dowry from Cordelia, and the Duke of Burgundy then decides he is no longer interested in her, the King of France proves his romantic love by his scornful words to Burgundy:

> Love's not love
>
> When it is mingled with regards that stands
>
> Aloof from the entire point. Will you have her?
>
> She is herself a dowry.   (I. 1. 241-244.)

A moment later he triumphantly takes possession of this feminine piece of jetsam, indeed a treasure trove, rightfully the property of a king. This delightful passage actually represents Shakespeare's handling of the love-theme more typically than Petruchio's practicality. Yet the dowry is probably always implied as part of the marriage in Shakespeare's plays, though it is over-

shadowed by the devotion of the lovers, even that of
Petruchio and Kate.

More striking than the custom of dowry, to modern
readers, is the confusion of marriage with pre-contract,
also called troth-plight, betrothal, and "handfasting."
This old custom was common in real life as may be observed in the life of Shakespeare and Anne Hathaway;
its convenience for dramatic plots led to its frequent appearance in plays. Though the doctrine of marriage as
a sacrament is an involved one, the central fact is this,
that for a valid marriage a man and woman make a contract with each other and confer the sacrament on each
other in the presence of witnesses. The requirement of
the Catholic Church and its successor the Anglican is
that a priest be one of the chief witnesses and that he
bless the marriage. But it is quite clear that in medieval
and Renaissance times the populace knew that a priest
was not indispensable for a valid marriage. Hence it
was that a ceremony of solemn betrothal before witnesses might too easily be regarded afterwards as a
marriage. Sometimes difficulty arose as to whether the
participants had pronounced *verba de futuro* or *verba
de praesenti* ("I, William, *will* take you, Anne," or "I,
William, *do* take you, Anne"). In fact, if a formal betrothal was followed by the use of marriage privileges,
the Church sometimes interpreted the act as proof of
the valid intention of marriage originally. Sometimes,
however, the couple might be condemned to do public
penance for incontinence.

As marriage and betrothal were so easily identified in
actual life, naturally dramatists frequently used the
confusion in plays. A handfasting (the origin of this
term for betrothal is obvious) could be represented as
having the binding force of a marriage contract. Elizabethan plays offer innumerable instances of plots turn-
ing on pre-contract, which is often supposed to have
occurred before the opening incident of the play. Flight
and pursuit, duels, lawsuits, the "bed-trick" of legally

substituting one woman for another, are some of the theatrical devices that are based on this ambiguity. Marriages are challenged as invalid and bigamous on the grounds of pre-contract to a third person by one of the parties. *Measure for Measure* is possibly Shakespeare's play most notable for dependence on pre-contract, as between Angelo and Mariana and between Claudio and Juliet. *Twelfth Night* shows Olivia leading Sebastian into a chapel to make a religious betrothal; she later calls him "husband," and the priest describes it as marriage (IV. 3. 22-35 and V. 1. 144-164). More typically, in the latter scene Orsino takes Viola's hand before witnesses, her brother and Olivia, in what is doubtless a betrothal (V. 1. 333-334). Similarly, France takes Cordelia's hand, in *King Lear* (I. 1. 255).

What has been said about popular and theatrical use of pre-contract may suggest that young people often fell in love and precipitated their union without waiting for parental consent. Though they sometimes did so, the fact does not nullify what has been said about marriages being arranged by families and dowries being necessary. For instance, in *Measure for Measure*, Claudio's marriage (not betrothal) to Juliet was delayed because of negotiation about the dowry (I. 2. 153-157); and Angelo broke his contract to Mariana because her dowry had been lost at sea (III. 1. 221-226). In less romantic dramatists than Shakespeare the pre-contract is sometimes a device to force the girl's father to provide a dowry, as well as his consent.

As contrasted with betrothed girls, widows were not involved in any special legalities on the Elizabethan stage. But it is worth noting here that a widow who had inherited most of her wealthy husband's estate became a prize and prey to all single men of any age, who immediately tried to inveigle her into a contract of marriage by any means, valid or fraudulent. Hence we are a little surprised that Falstaff does not marry Dame Quickly, when she becomes a widow between Parts 1 and

II of *Henry* IV. She and her tavern appear to provide the kind of refuge from honest effort which Falstaff is looking for. But in fact she "serves his uses both in purse and in person" without the restraints of marriage (Part II, II. 1. 124-127). He is funnier as her deluder than he would be as her hen-pecked spouse. Furthermore, Sir John is a gentleman and still aspires to Prince Hal's favor. So Ancient Pistol wins "the quondam Quickly."

Marriage was the only recognized vocation for women in Renaissance England. But even though excluded from the professions of politics, law, the ministry, and medicine, women surely played as important a part in the world (not merely in "society") as they do now. Many women shared with their husbands the decisions required in administering great estates. Widows, both of aristocrats and of tradesmen, often accepted the full responsibility of managing an estate or a business. However, unlike other dramatists of the age, Shakespeare does not often present bourgeois life in his plays. If he had, he would have shown the social importance of the rich merchant's or tradesman's widow, who wielded her wealth and sex to great advantage for herself and her family. Marriage may indeed have been the only accepted place for women, but in expectation of it and within it they played for power and pride equally with men.

Lady Portia, in *The Merchant of Venice,* is of course not a widow, but the daughter of a father who has left her very wealthy; his will, however, prescribes the device of the caskets to determine the man who shall be her husband. But Portia's words leave a strong implication that she does not have to give to every man who presents himself as a suitor the privilege of trying his wits on the caskets. He must first be acceptable to her as a potential husband (see I. 2. 24-29, 116-119; II. 1. 13-16). In fact, why should Bassanio borrow so much money from Antonio if it were not to make a splendid

impression on the Lady of Belmont? In *Twelfth Night*
the Countess Olivia is another such independent heiress,
though her prudence is not so striking as Portia's.

Parent and child

We know that in medieval and Renaissance times
the parents' authority over the child seemed more abso-
lute than it does today. But the number of elopements
and secret marriages shows that the spirit of youth was
the same then as now. Apparently parental authority,
at least among gentlefolk, the class with which Shakespeare chiefly deals, was exerted mainly through its control of inheritance. Our generation, which normally ex-
pects each man to make his own fortune, is struck by
the dependence of Elizabethan sons and daughters upon
their inherited "portions." Since a gentleman was ordinarily one who lived on the income from his property,
especially land, without working at a profession, we
should not be surprised at an Elizabethan young man's
reluctance to endanger his position by defiance of his
parents. He had more at stake than just a comfortable
living. A gentleman was at least potentially an officer in
the army or a statesman; he enjoyed the respect and
acceptance of his youthful peers in the governing class.
He had been trained only in the etiquette of the court,
the management of great estates, and the skills of bearing arms, hunting, dancing, and singing or playing on
an instrument. If he had attended university or an Inn
of Court, he had had a more or less thorough tutoring
in the liberal arts, possibly some knowledge of the law.
Obviously, he was neither equipped nor willing to cast
aside all the advantages of his life, even for the love of
a pretty but portionless girl, and submit himself to
seven years' toilsome apprenticeship to an artisan or
merchant. In *The Winter's Tale* when Prince Florizel
defies his father and runs away with a shepherd's daughter, we see that we are far in the realm of romance. As

a matter of fact, we have known all along that she is
really a castaway princess.

While understanding the economic and social means
of parental control, we need not forget that reverence
for age and parents was then more emphatically taught
in the home and the church. But the effect of the teaching is hard to gauge, for the formulas of respect are not
certain indications of real feeling. But the social power
of inheritance is an evident fact.

Honor among men and women

As has been said above, part of a gentleman's
advantages in the world was the respect due him by
birth. The word *respect* does not really convey all the
deference and prestige accorded to an Elizabethan aristocrat; he himself called it "honor." A number of books
about honor and its defence in the duel were published
in the late sixteenth and early seventeenth centuries,
and from them we learn that honor was of two origins,
indicated by the terms *native honor* and *acquired honor*.
Most gentlemen who were entitled to honor by birth
usually retained it through life. They could add to it
and perfect it by deeds of valor on the battlefield or in
the lists or by rendering notably good counsel or diplo-
matic service to their king, that is, by statesmanship.
Thus they acquired honor. A commoner also could acquire honor by similar means and for his achievement
was usually ennobled by his king and raised to gentility.

Possession of honor meant acceptance by the nobility
as an equal; it meant that advantageous marriages, as
well as splendid careers at court or in the army, were
possible for one's children. While traveling abroad, the
gentleman was received by Continental aristocrats with
honor suitable to his rank, and he saw the best of culture and luxury that foreign capitals could offer. To be
a man of honor meant that one's "word" was accepted
as good. But it must be said at once that many men

technically honorable were guilty of vile deceits and acts
that seem to us most dishonorable.

For honor in our sense — that is, integrity, truth,
and a keen sense of justice — often were completely
lacking in men who passed as gentlemen in Elizabethan
society. Lord Robert Dudley, later Earl of Leicester
and Elizabeth's favorite, cheated a kinsman named John
Littleton by selling him at a high price a piece of property part of which had already been devised to Dudley's
wife, Lady Anne. Though modern historians are doubtful, Leicester's contemporaries believed he was accessory
to the murder of Lady Anne ("Amy Robsart"). He
afterwards married and then repudiated Lady Douglas
Sheffield. By refusing to acknowledge the marriage, he
confirmed their son Robert in bastardy.[2] Yet Leicester
was doubtless a "man of honor." Obviously, brazen ar-
rogance enabled such a man to escape direct challenge.

How was the honor of a gentleman lost? Most dra-
matically, by conviction of treason. If a person of title
was attainted of treason, he must stand trial by his
peers in the House of Lords or submit to trial by ordeal,
in the form of a combat conducted under martial law in
the lists. If defeated in the combat or found guilty in
court, the traitor lost his life under the axe, forfeited
his possessions to the Crown, and lost all honor. Much
worse — his wife and children lost honor, too. Im-
poverished and degenerate, the widow was unable to
rear her children in conditions proper to their ancestry
or to marry them in their class when they came of age.
The family were dependent on the pity of relatives or
of the King. It is not surprising that many gentlemen
charged with treason simply refused to plead either
guilty or not guilty; then they could not be tried. But
to force them to plead, they could be, and were, pressed
by heavy weights, a torture called the *peine forte et
dure*. If they endured silent until death, their families
were not subject to the penalties of attaint of treason.

[2] Hubert Hall, *Society in the Elizabethan Age,* 1902, pp. 92-94.

Shakespeare uses many of these legal and social aspects of honor to strong dramatic effect in *Richard* II.

Less extraordinary was the loss of honor privately through cowardice, petty treason, or other offenses. In all of these dishonor hinged upon the giving and the acceptance, or the repelling, of the lie. In brief, the protocol was as follows: If one gentleman suspected another of doing him an injury (say cheating at dice, slandering his good name, or seducing his wife), he accused his enemy of the offense, or of another offense dishonorable to a gentleman, or he gave him a blow. If the enemy refused to resent the insult, he was proved a coward and without honor. Ordinarily he returned the affront by accusing his adversary of lying (or he returned the blow, was called a base fellow, and gave the lie). The receiver of the lie then challenged his enemy to a duel. Arrangements for time, place, and weapons were made by seconds. The Defender, who in the protocol was always he who had given the lie, had the privilege of choosing the weapons. The Challenger, that is, he who originally felt himself injured, had to kill or at least disarm his enemy in the duel; if the Defender successfully warded off the attack, the Challenger was convicted of the lie and lost honor. Naturally, if the Defender was beaten, he lost his honor.[3]

A gentleman who lost honor through cowardice in a quarrel or defeat in a duel was obviously not so badly off as one convicted of treason by the law, for the law did not permit private duels. Hence the defeated duelist was not likely to lose his property. Theoretically, he should have lost it; the code of honor, which herein followed the martial law, yielded all of the vanquished man's goods to the victor. But since the private duel was outside the civil and martial law of the realm, the victor

[3] The protocol is given in detail in such works as Sir William Segar, *The Booke of Honor and Armes,* 1590, and *Vincentio Saviolo his Practise,* 1595, which Shakespeare parodies in *As You Like It,* V. 4. 44-108.

could not use legal action to acquire the conquered one's estates. Still the social penalties of dishonor were heavy, if we can believe the writers on honor. The defeated man was not to be received by members of his class; if insulted, he gave the lie in vain, for no man of honor was obliged to credit him or deal with him. His children also lost honor. It is doubtful if the social consequences were as severe as the theorists believed that they should be. But among young gallants defeat in a duel might seem a catastrophe, an eternal disgrace, and this attitude lends meaning to many episodes in Shakespeare, notably the duels in *Romeo and Juliet*. It even lies behind Miranda's warning to Prospero not to insult her lover Ferdinand any more:

> O dear father,
> Make not too rash a trial of him, for
> He's gentle and not fearful.
> *(The Tempest*, I. 2. 466-468.)

By *gentle* she means 'a man of honor.' Thirst for acquired honor makes Guiderius and Arviragus discontented mountaineers in the Welsh wilderness; for, unknown to themselves, they are princes. Their fosterfather Belarius comments:

> 'Tis wonder
> That an invisible instinct should frame them
> To royalty unlearn'd, honour untaught,
> Civility not seen from other, valour
> That wildly grows in them but yields a crop
> As if it had been sow'd.
> *(Cymbeline*, IV. 2. 176-181.)

Gentlewomen also possessed native honor, usually called "honesty." This they could lose only by unchastity. But a married woman's loss of honor was more than personal disgrace; it was deeply criminal, for it imperiled the honor of husband and children. Feminine infidelity led to doubt about the paternity of the children. Since bastards were born without honor and were excluded from inheritance by law, the consequences of a mother's unchastity were disastrous. This special importance of adultery is not, of course, the primary cause of agony for Hamlet and Othello, who are anguished most of all by discovering that a being whom they had worshipped is vile. But the personal loss of honor for themselves is also an actual cause of pain. Modern critics sometimes scorn the emphasis on "technical virtue" in women of the Elizabethan drama, as if the Elizabethans overlooked the loveliness of goodness for goodness' sake. However, the preceding discussion of marriage and of honor has indicated that the society in which Shakespeare lived relied on a set of legal conventions different from our own. Points of view differ. The ease with which divorce can be obtained and the softness with which criminals are treated today would have shocked Elizabethans to their souls. Possibly they loved virtue for its own sake or for the love of God as much as we do.

Society and government

Among the ways in which the Elizabethan view of the world contrasts to our own we should note its basic assumption of permanence in the order of things. Today evolutionary theory and scientific achievement have accustomed us to constant change in matter, in biological form, and even in human society. Most people of Shakespeare's time, however, viewed the world as composed of permanent, unvarying kinds and orders of created things. Created beings were thought of as ranked in hierarchies of value and importance, called degrees. Inanimate materials themselves revealed this order, for instance, the degrees of nobility in metals from lead to gold, of beauty in gems, of power in the stars and planets. More comprehensible to us was the hierarchy of value in living creatures, from the tiniest worm to the cherub, highest in rank among the nine choirs of angels.

The "great chain of being," then, rises in innumerable links, or degrees, from the dust of earth to God Himself, the infinite source of all things. Each class of beings, material or spiritual, has its value, its duty, so to speak, in God's creation. Inanimate creatures like water, cannot, of course, fail in their function or violate order and degree except when driven by impulses from outside themselves; nor can beasts, which are animate but irrational beings, create discord. Only spiritual beings, that is, men and angels, gifted with reason, can set their wills against the Almighty's and break the divine order of Creation. Fundamentally, of course, they do so by breaking the moral order; Satan was the prime source of all discord when he defied the will of God. But men also constantly shatter the concord of society by violating

> degree, priority, and place,
> Insisture [regularity], course, proportion, season,
>   form,
> Office, and custom, in all line of order . . .
> The primogenitive and due of birth,
> Prerogative of age, crowns, sceptres, laurels . . .
>   (*Troilus and Cressida*, I. 3. 86-88, 106-107.)

To put this idea another way, each group, rank, and position in human society has its functions, responsibilities, and rights. Society is a complex organization in which each part must be respected and guarded. Injustice violates the rights and functions of an element of society and endangers the divinely planned order of human relations and even that of all nature. To cite a humble example, if a monopolist were to raise the price of tin so that tinkers could not afford to follow their trade, a necessary work in society would be destroyed and discord would jar human life. A more spectacular instance was plain in Tudor society. Wealthy financiers bought and enclosed large tracts of agricultural land for purposes of sheep-raising; they violently disordered society by moving thousands of tenants off the soil that their ancestors had tilled for centuries, turned them into beggars and thieves because of lack of work, and raised the price of food through the scarcity of farm produce which resulted. These economic evils may appear to originate in the sin of avarice, rather than in violations of order. But basically order is violated because the monopolist or the financier is striving for greater wealth or splendor of life than his social place assigns him, for instance, as a courtier or a goldsmith. Violations of degree, then, are measured by the human suffering which results. If men's immoral disregard of rank and right grows unchecked, it ends in mere savagery:

> . . . an universal wolf . . .
>
> Must make perforce an universal prey,
>
> And last eat up himself.

(Troilus and Cressida, I. 3. 121-124.)

As Shakespeare says in another part of this same speech, the planets themselves, if thought of as ruled by spirits, may "to disorder wander" and by discord in heaven produce raging seas and earthquakes, as well as lesser disasters. Conversely, disorders in human society may provoke disturbance in the heavenly bodies, meant as warnings, protests, or punishment for human crime. The correspondence of social and celestial discord is frequently stressed in Shakespeare's plays, notably in *Julius Caesar* and *Macbeth*.

This brief statement of the doctrine of order may leave the student with the impression that Shakespeare was utterly "medieval" in his thinking and wished every man to be fettered in the niche in society in which he happened to be born. The conclusion is unjust. Shakespeare's thought was of the necessity of safeguarding all authority and law and the reverence due to them; for they come from God and constitute the foundation of peace and of any happiness to be found in human society. When a man goes beyond the scope of his established social right and function, he at once violates the authority of another. Yet Shakespeare could clearly perceive that a man might raise himself to higher honor and power by energetic use of his talents, always with strict regard to the authority and rights of all men. Unfortunately, such integrity is so rare that it is almost never seen. Sir Thomas More, who was born a lawyer's son and became Lord Chancellor of England, was certainly proof that such heroic virtue could exist. But More's predecessor as Chancellor, Cardinal Thomas Wolsey, who was born son of a butcher, was seen by Elizabethans, apparently including Shakespeare, as the very type of the "ambitious" man — proud, greedy, vindictive, cunning, tyrannical. Thus he is dramatized in *Henry* VIII; what his character was in fact is not important in this connection. Shakespeare's dramas which deal with historical contests for power in the state naturally provide him with many opportunities to depict the consequent evils of disorder. This philosophic view deepens the tragic feeling of the plays and at times even serves for tragic irony, as in the instance of the Bishop of Carlisle's prophecy, in *Richard* II (IV. 1. 115-149). The careers of Bolingbroke (in the same play and the two parts of *Henry* IV) and of Macbeth are eminent examples of the lust for power and its tragic results for the state.

Let us glance briefly at the Elizabethan conception of kingship. Since the feudal levels of English society have lasted into the twentieth century, we can understand how natural was Shakespeare's assumption that a feudal pattern was the permanent, God-given form for society and government. At the top of the pyramid was the sovereign, God's vice-gerent, who had been solemnly anointed by the chief priest of the Anglican Church, using consecrated oils. The King was the chief executive of the state and the ultimate source of justice in the courts of law. The maxim that "the king can do no wrong" was not true of the sovereign as a private man, of course, and even as king he could be tyrannical or cruel. But the maxim protected the office or function of the sovereign against the courts of law and Parliament. If the commons were exasperated beyond endurance by the Crown's demands for money, Parliament could severely punish the King's ministers — *they* had violated the law, not the King. Richard II is never really tried for his crimes in Parliament; rather, he finds his subjects determinedly rebellious, and in despair he submits to their will and abdicates. His counselors are executed for having misled their King. Richard is slain by a murderer, not by the arm of the law.

It also suited the Tudor monarchs, from Henry VII through Elizabeth, to propagate the doctrine of "passive obedience." When a sovereign's rule seemed to the subjects to be tyrannical and unjust, they should remember the divine source of the royal power, that kings are sent by God to rule states; and the people should submit, praying God to lead the King's heart to better ways and to forgive them the sins which had brought the punishment of oppression. Passive obedience was always better than armed rebellion or resistance, which divides a country into warring factions and offends the Almighty by contempt for his delegated authority. This doctrine was developed to counter any dangerous theories, some of them medieval in origin, about the authority of the sovereign having been delegated to him by the people originally, by whom it might be taken back or transferred to another person. Passive obedience was taught, let us note, from the pulpits of the English

Church, for after Henry VIII, the King was the head of the Church.

Passive obedience was supported by fear generated by recent events. The Wars of the Roses, between the factions of the houses of York and Lancaster, had occupied almost the third quarter of the fifteenth century and had given the English people endless examples of the bloodshed and waste of feudal strife. Henry VII, born Henry Tudor, claimed that the two families were united in his own blood and person and by his marriage to Elizabeth of York; nevertheless, he was constantly anxious about rebellion and had to raise armies several times to crush discontented peasantry or Yorkist partisans. In the sixteenth century the reigns of Henry VIII, Edward, Mary, and Elizabeth, especially Elizabeth's long rule (1558-1603), witnessed several dangerous conspiracies and insurrections. Repeated threats of Spanish invasion increased the danger that would lie in civil war. All in all, it is not surprising that Shakespeare mentions civil war with horror and fully accepts passive obedience. The doctrine is expressed in many of his plays. It is implicit in *Julius Caesar*, for the Elizabethans interpreted Brutus's share in the assassination as a desperate mistake of his political judgment which inevitably wracked his country with "domestic fury and fierce civil strife." [4] The bitterest taunt that Octavius and Antony throw at Brutus at the meeting before Philippi is *traitor* (V. 1. 55-57, 64; III. 1. 263-264).

On the other hand, Shakespeare clearly expressed the ideal of a good king. In *Macbeth* Malcolm enumerates a formidable list of "the king-becoming graces"; there are twelve of these virtues, nine more than Holinshed's *Chronicle* says that Malcolm spoke of. Though he does not claim them all as his own, Malcolm is exalted as a hero fully virtuous enough for the redemption of Scot-

[4] See the discussion by J. Leeds Barroll, "Shakespeare and Roman History," *Modern Language Review*, LIII (1958), 326-343.

land from degenerate Macbeth. In contrast, Richard II is obviously unfit for his high office; and his rival, Bolingbroke, though a brave, determined, intelligent man, usurps the throne and instigates the murder of Richard. Shakespeare saw the problem just as well as we believe we see it at this distance: Royal blood and coronation oils do not endue a man with either wisdom or virtue. Erasmus and other Renaissance thinkers also saw it and, as a partial solution, wrote instructions on the proper education of a Christian prince. Obviously, wise counselors and ministers can curb the evil that a foolish or vicious king may aim to do; therefore, Christian religion and humanistic education must leaven the aristocracy and through them influence the king. Essentially, the success of modern democratic government depends on extending the same foundations throughout the masses.

However, in any political reference Shakespeare almost invariably speaks of the lower classes with contempt. He certainly never conceived of any genuinely democratic political system. Yet his disparagement of the rabble is partly due to his using the conventional language of educated men when speaking of the uneducated. Ben Jonson, son of a bricklayer and himself bred to that trade, talks of

> The eager multitude (who never yet
>
> Knew why to love or hate, but only pleas'd
>
> T'express their rage of power).
>
> (*Sejanus*, V. 759-761.)[5]

Spencer calls the people the "rascal rabblement." To expect Shakespeare, with all his humanity, to take an optimistic view of the political wisdom of the common people would be to expect him to anticipate by two centuries campaigns for universal education and a revo-

[5] The line numbers are those used in *Ben Jonson,* ed. Herford and Simpson, vol. IV (1932).

lutionary view of the common man. Far closer to him than these things was the Peasants' Revolt of 1384.

The humors, the stars, and human character

Before speaking of the physiological and psychological humors, it may be wise to offer a word of caution. In any age, whether the sixteenth or the twentieth century, only a very naive person could believe that human behavior may truly be interpreted by means of narrow formulas like "drives," "complexes," or "humors." Shakespeare did not think so. Therefore, we should not assume that when we have learned the four humors, we have the key to his characters.

However, there are frequent references to humors in his plays, and sometimes his persons manifest the symptoms of a dominant humor. It follows that we should have a concept of what the humors were. According to Greek physics, the primary qualities of all matter are heat, cold, dryness, and moisture. The humors of the human body are four fluid substances produced by the digestion of food in the stomach and liver; and each of the four possesses two of the primary qualities. *Blood* is hot and moist; *choler* (or bile) is hot and dry; *phlegm* is cold and moist; *melancholy* (or black bile) is cold and dry. (That a fluid substance could be cold and dry may be imagined on the analogy of a concentrated acid.) Each of the humors has its function and its organ of operation or reception. The blood, which warms the whole body and is transmuted into flesh, heated by the heart gives off vital spirits to enliven the body. Choler assists in excretion and gathers in the gall bladder. Phlegm nourishes the brain, although its gathering places are the kidneys and lungs. Melancholy nourishes bones and sinews; its surplus is received in the spleen. All human bodies of course generate these humors in some proportion. In a person of "good humor" or good "complexion," as the Elizabethans said, the four humors are in effective balance for health and happiness.

If by chance one humor becomes preponderant, the person's disposition is affected in such a way as to manifest the typical qualities of the humor. If blood predominates, a sanguine disposition appears, unusually energetic, courageous, hopeful, and sensuous. If the man is choleric (or bilious), he is proud, irritable, prone to anger, quarrelsome, and ambitious. If phlegm is dominant, he is slow of response, unemotional, dull. If he is melancholy, he is gloomy, silent, apprehensive, morose, and solitary. The humors also reveal characteristic hues in the skin: the sanguine, ruddy; the choleric, yellowish; the phlegmatic, pale; and the melancholy, swarthy or grayish.

Unfortunately, human beings are not born (it was believed) with balanced temperaments or proportions of humors, but rather with a proneness to the dominance of one. And whichever humor is in surplus may also be fostered by one's own habits and behavior. For instance, he may increase choler by allowing anger to master him too often. He may create excessive black bile by devotion to sedentary or solitary occupations, e.g., study or meditation. He may increase phlegm by drinking too much milk. Thus, habits, diet, and occupation may be indulged to the point of altering one's humor for the worse. On the other hand, the same means may be used for diminishing a "peccant humor." By accepting the guidance of a physician, one may regain health through following prescriptions for a better diet and perhaps more exercise and a change of scene. However, the universal first step to reduce the surplus humor was bleeding, for much of the offending substance was thus taken away at once. Purging the bowels was thought to have the same good effect.

It is clear that the humor dominant in a man inclines him to certain passions — except that the phlegmatic is passionless and dull. Excessive blood leads to lust;

choler, to anger; melancholy, to fear and sorrow. The passions are both the cause and the result of a dominant humor. So control of the passions is important for health. In fact, control is made even more necessary by the fact that prolonged violent passion acts somehow to convert any dominant humor into a specially noxious form called *humor adust* (from the Latin *ad-ustum*, 'burnt up'). Humor adust is so damaging to the system that disease and death are likely soon to follow. Indeed all humors are consumed to this dry form called melancholy adust. Whether Hamlet's humor has reached adustion may be doubtful, but there is no question that he indulged his melancholy too long and to the point of suicidal wishes.

Love, the universal passion, in Shakespeare is one of the most entertaining; for the dramatist does not present its psychical dangers at all gravely. Lovers' melancholy, which other playwrights depict seriously, Shakespeare's lovers unconsciously assume as a pose; they discard it at once when real emotion grips them. While they are affecting love-melancholy, they are viewed ironically. In this light we see Romeo before he meets Juliet and Orsino while he is trying to woo Olivia, in *Twelfth Night*.

During the Renaissance the physiology of humors and the ancient science of astrology were closely correlated. This was inevitable. Because the sun and moon meteorologically affect the elements of our planet, the fluids of the body necessarily change under their power. But it was a much more radical idea, both scientifically and philosophically, to ascribe a special effect upon the humors to each star, planet, and sign in the heavens. The celestial bodies, by their power of generating excessive humor or of corrupting humor, "incline" human beings to certain passions and appetites. Thus they control human life. Very few of the astrologers dared to say that the astral influence was irresistible, but all admitted its great potency. Further, since at the moment of birth the conjunction of the heavenly bodies and their influence could be determined for the child's whole life, this knowledge should be of medical value. When a physician visited a patient, he was likely to want to know his horoscope before beginning treatment, perhaps even before diagnosis. In fact most physicians were to some degree astrologers; many astrologers also practiced medicine.

Because of the close association of physiology and astrology, they are frequently mentioned together. As today a man interests himself in the quirks of his health and prescribes iodine or vitamins for himself following what he reads in the health column of the newspaper, so in Shakespeare's age the average man knew his horoscope and more or less seriously respected his stars and their influence on his temperament.

Probably everyone in the Elizabethan age accepted the physiology of humors as basically true; but there was much debate about astrology. From the early centuries the Catholic Church had denounced it, yet several Renaissance Popes maintained astrologers. Melancthon and Cardan accepted the science, Calvin and Agrippa rejected it. Anglican divines frequently wrote against it. How many of Shakespeare's audience in the Globe Theater had a firm faith in the influence of the stars, how many were uncertain, it is impossible to estimate. However, by Edmund's jeers at astrology in *King Lear*, I. 2. 127-145, Shakespeare achieved a double dramatic value: Everyone was amused by the villain's satiric wit, yet most were shocked by his unbelief. For when coupled with his earlier assertion, "Thou, Nature, art my goddess," his skepticism about the stars' influence suggests a grosser materialism; he seems to reject all supersensible reality. Doubtless he is an atheist as well as a Machiavellian.

The Elizabethans, then, like ourselves, tried to reconcile somewhat contradictory ideas about human nature. Latent in the psychology of the humors and in astrology was mechanistic determinism. It could not, however, be allowed to supersede the truths of free-will, moral responsibility, and a Divine Providence responsive to human prayer. Christianity and the teachings of ancient philosophers still provided the basic patterns of thought. Yet even the most learned and pious mind sometimes found the course of human life a tragic enigma. The student must keep these conflicts of doctrine in mind and avoid the blunder of interpreting Shakespeare's characters superficially.

4

Shakespeare's Career

IN THIS CHAPTER we shall first glance at the established facts of Shakespeare's life and then attempt to survey his career as a writer.

The student who reads two or three biographical accounts of Shakespeare discovers that the known facts of the dramatist's life are so few they can be set down in several paragraphs. Book-length biographies of Shakespeare are amplified principally by two methods: 1] providing the reader with elaborate description of the social and theatrical environment in which Shakespeare lived and worked, and 2] speculating about Shakespeare's probable movements and activities. Both of these efforts are legitimate ones for scholars; but they do not provide us with more events of the dramatist's life.

On the other hand, the scarcity of known facts for Shakespeare's biography must not be given undue importance. We notice the scarcity only if we compare biographies of modern men with that of Shakespeare. The truth is that in his era, biographies of contemporary literary men were rare; persons of less importance than kings, statesmen, prelates, and martyrs were seldom the subjects of published biography. Indeed we know as much about Shakespeare's life as about the lives of some men more celebrated than he in his own time (for instance, John Donne), because of the exhaustive search for facts about Shakespeare in later centuries. Researchers have turned up enough data from legal records and theater documents to provide indisputable outlines of his career and proof of his authorship of the plays that pass under his name. No first-rate scholar has ever accepted the evidence offered by the Baconians or others who argue that Shakespeare did not write the dramas that his fellow-actors, Heminge and Condell, published as his.

William Shakespeare was probably born about April 24, 1564, in Stratford-on-Avon, in Warwickshire, a middle county (examine a map of England). We know only the precise date of his baptism, April 26. But we also know that since in those times a great many infants died soon after birth, babies were often christened within a few days of their arrival. William was the second child of John and Mary Arden Shakespeare. The baptism was recorded in Holy Trinity Church register.

The father, John, came of good yeoman stock and was a dealer in leather goods, including gloves, and in wool. He prospered for many years and became a leading citizen of Stratford; in 1565-1587 he was an alderman, in 1568 bailiff (mayor). Finally, in 1596 he (or rather his son William for him) applied to the Herald's Office for the grant of a coat of arms, to serve as final proof that he was a "gentleman." The arms were granted. But ever since 1577, for reasons that are now obscure, John Shakespeare's prosperity had waned.

In 1592 he was cited to the ecclesiastical court for recusancy, the offense of non-attendance at services in the Established Church in the parish to which one belonged. Since after John's death a book of Catholic devotion, bearing his signature, and his testament, made according to a Catholic formula, were found in his house, it has been suspected that John had become a Catholic. This theory receives further support from the fact that his wife, born Mary Arden, belonged to an old county family which had clung steadily to Catholicism, despite the legal penalties of the Reformation time. It is probable that Mary remained a faithful though secret Catholic throughout her life, and that she drew her husband into her faith. That William was baptized by a minister of the Church of England does not oppose the idea of Mary's Catholicism; for Catholics frequently permitted the sacrament to be administered by an Anglican cleric, partly to escape legal penalties for not doing so, partly because of the scarcity of their own priests. All in all, it seems likely that the dramatist's sympathy with some doctrines and forms of the old faith, as they are evidenced in his plays, had its source in Catholic training as a boy.

William Shakespeare's boyhood and schooling must have been outwardly much like those of other sons of prosperous tradesmen. In 1709 Nicholas Rowe, a dramatist acquainted with actors who may have preserved old traditions, said that Shakespeare was educated at a free-school, i.e., municipal school. It has always been assumed, and seems very likely, that this was Stratford Grammar School. He probably attended from about the age of seven (after elementary training in a "petty" school) and continued in Grammar School for eight or ten years. Stratford School paid a good salary and employed for the headmastership a succession of men trained at Oxford, one of whom was a Master of Arts. An usher was appointed to assist the headmaster with the younger pupils. The curriculum consisted almost wholly of Latin grammar, Latin composition (oral and written), and Latin literature; the older pupils aiming at University fellowships may have learned the elements of Greek. The textbooks included selections or complete works by the moralist and satirist Erasmus; the poets Ovid, Horace, Virgil, and Mantuan; the dramatists Seneca and Terence; the orator and philosopher Cicero; the historians Caesar and Sallust. This education was at least comparable with a modern college major in classics. Ben Jonson described Shakespeare's learning as being "small Latin and less Greek." But this disparagement implies that for "much" Latin Shakespeare ought to have had five more years of university study of the classics, culminating in an M.A. degree.

Nicholas Rowe also asserted that John Shakespeare withdrew William from school to assist his father in his trade of dealing in wool. Whether he was apprenticed to his father or (as Rowe says) "to a butcher" who was not his father, we have no information beyond uncertain tradition. We may, however, be sure that the knowledge of hawking, hunting, and archery, of horses, dogs, and wild things, of peddlers, shepherds, and farmfolk — this store of information in his plays and poems was not acquired only from books, but indicates a normal freedom to roam the countryside and enjoy himself. Three commentators of the seventeenth century, as well as Rowe, mention the Stratford tradition that Shakespeare killed deer in the preserves of Sir Thomas Lucy at Charlecote and was prosecuted by that gentleman. The story has been rejected by some scholars. Unquestionably there is a satiric joke against the Lucys, possibly against Sir Thomas, in *The Merry Wives of Windsor*; and deer stealing is mentioned in the same episode (I. 1).

There is no legal record of Shakespeare between his baptism and his marriage to Anne Hathaway. Anne seems to have been eight years older than Shakespeare. The ecclesiastical license for the marriage was issued on 27 November, 1582. Though record of the actual ceremony (evidently in some other parish than Stratford) has not been found, there is no reason to doubt that it was performed, perhaps at Temple Grafton, a hamlet given as Anne's home in the license. But in fact Anne's family lived at Shottery, a community in the large parish of Holy Trinity centered in Stratford. There is a little mystery here, as there is in the reason for haste in the marriage. The bishop of Worcester's permission was sought and granted for performing the marriage after one proclamation of the banns, contrary to church law, which requires three. Inevitably we explain the hasty marriage by the fact that Anne was pregnant, for a daughter of William and Anne was baptized on 26 May, 1583. Not uncommonly in those times, couples who had made a formal betrothal considered it to be a marriage, although the Church insisted upon a public religious ceremony. It may be, then, that "pre-contract," as social custom, partly excuses Shakespeare and Anne.

Following the first child, Susanna, twins named Hamnet and Judith were born in 1585. Hamnet died in 1596, but the daughters lived to a ripe age. There were no other children.

The years between 1584 and 1592 are a blank in the biography except for the baptism of Hamnet and Judith. A prominent actor who was born in the early seventeenth century told the biographer John Aubrey that Shakespeare in his younger years was "a schoolmaster in the country." The dramatist has also been identified with a provincial actor named William Shakeshaft, mentioned in 1581 in Lancashire. Either or both of these traditions may be true.

The date of Shakespeare's arrival in London is also uncertain. But by 1592 he was well enough known in the metropolis to be sneered at in a book by a rival dramatist. Robert Greene said that Shakespeare, the "upstart crow," thought himself "the only Shake-scene in a country." The reference is almost unique in its ill nature; invariably other references speak of Shakespeare as amiable. We do not know how Shakespeare began in the world of the theater. He may have come from his schoolmastering with one or two plays to sell to the London actors. He may have begun as an apprentice actor with a London company, perhaps the Lord Strange's Men or the Earl of Pembroke's Men.

Greene's spiteful description implies that the actor-playwright had made himself a too-successful rival to Greene, a process that would require a year or more. Recently, some scholars have argued for dating the composition of Shakespeare's early plays in the middle 1580's. We do not know exactly when they were first written or produced.

Certain it is that from 1594 until his retirement, Shakespeare remained with one company, first known as the Lord Chamberlain's, then as the King's Company (after the accession of King James I, 1603). At first it was rivaled in importance by one of the several other groups in London, the Lord Admiral's Men, which included the great tragedian, Edward Alleyn. But through the rise to greatness of Richard Burbage, their own tragedian, the Chamberlain's Men attained supremacy and kept it until Parliament ended all Elizabethan drama by an ordinance closing the theaters, on the brink of the Civil War in 1642. Therefore, it is clear that Shakespeare enjoyed the advantage of the best actors available for his plays; and in turn he gave the company success by the power of his drama. The company owned two theaters, at first the large, open-air, public one called the Globe in Southwark, on the south bank of the Thames, and later (besides the Globe) the smaller, enclosed, "private" Blackfriars, in the city. The Globe is the theater for which Shakespeare's greatest plays were written. The Blackfriars was used by the company only from 1609 on, and only in the winter season.

Besides writing plays, Shakespeare acted in his own and other men's at least until 1603, and possibly later. Ben Jonson includes Shakespeare's name in the list of actors for *Every Man in His Humour* and *Sejanus*, acted in 1598 and 1603. But by the latter date Shakespeare had also been for nine years a "sharer" in the Chamberlain's Men. As such he derived his share of income from the box-office of the Globe, just as he paid his share of the expenses. Because of his triple capacity as dramatist, actor, and sharer, Shakespeare may be considered as a successful businessman. As early as 1597 he had purchased a "substantial" house, called New Place, in Stratford. We know of a few other of his business transactions. His fellow-members of the Company such as John Heminge, Richard Burbage, and Henry Condell, were also well-to-do property owners and respected citizens.

The years in London were probably broken by visits of varying length in Stratford. In the several records of Shakespeare's legal residences in London, his wife is not mentioned. Of course she may have been with him there; or she and the daughters may have remained in their original home. Shakespeare's father died in 1601, but his mother lived until 1608. All these facts combined suggest that the playwright may have returned fairly often to his native town ("once a year," says Aubrey). The tenant to whom Shakespeare rented New Place seems to have been expected to vacate the house in 1610; therefore, it may be, as Sir Edmund Chambers believes, that from 1610 on Shakespeare spent most of his time in Stratford, though he contributed a few plays to his company after that year. Shakespeare's actual playwriting may have ended in 1611 or 1612. From time to time he visited London. His last years in Stratford were uneventful. One tradition gives as the cause of his death that he died of a fever contracted from heavy drinking at a "merry meeting" with the poets Ben Jonson and Michael Drayton, old acquaintances. Another account mentions that he died a Catholic. He died on 23 April 1616, possibly on his birthday.

Shakespeare's hope that his property might pass to a long line of descendants is apparent in his will; but it was in vain, for his only grandchild died in 1670, without offspring.

THE PRECEDING PARAGRAPHS have given all the major facts known about Shakespeare's life. That they are given at all and that you are asked to know them implies that they relate, perhaps only distantly, to our understanding and appreciation of Shakespeare's writings. On the contrary, some critics have maintained that any literary work should be appreciated with complete independence of its author's life — let the work speak for itself. Without entering into a discussion of this critical problem, let us only note that for the undergraduate there are unquestionable advantages in using biographical information, at least in the *approach* to criticism. For instance, the student profits from understanding the kind of schooling which Shakespeare had and the scope of his study of Latin literature. Equipped with this biographical information, one reads such plays as *The Comedy of Errors* and *Julius Caesar*, as well as *Venus and Adonis* and *The Rape of Lucrece*, without false impressions of either the poet's originality or his deep historical scholarship. Consequently, one is readier to see and evaluate actual literary distinctions in these works. It would be even better, of course, to read Plautus's, Plutarch's, and Ovid's masterpieces before studying Shakespeare. However, even a general notion of their place in the education of a sixteenth century Englishman is of some value to any reader of Shakespeare.

On the other hand, it is important to emphasize that the events of Shakespeare's life have very few direct, important connections with his plays — perhaps none at all that can be demonstrated. The student should bear in mind, while reading the paragraphs that follow, that simple inferences about the connections of the dramatist's life with his plays are very dangerous, for they ignore many other kinds of influence on Shakespeare, for instance, his own temperament, changing dramatic fashions, the changes in the personnel of the King's Men, the competition of rival companies, the political situation in England, and the literary tastes of the sovereign. Besides this basic complexity of influence, we are also hampered by the fact that our knowledge of the dates of the plays is not precise. The kinds of evidence which lead to a hypothetical chronology of Shakespeare's works are discussed in Chapter 5. Now, by means of the kind of evidence cited in Chapter 5 it is possible to arrange Shakespeare's plays in a sequence of the approximate dates of composition (see Column I of the "Chronology," Chapter 6). Looking over this sequence, the scholar sees Shakespeare's career as a dramatist somewhat as it is described in the following paragraphs.

When young Shakespeare came to London, he found a lively medley of theatrical activity and a rapidly developing drama. However, certain dramatists and certain genres stood out. John Lyly was producing witty, fantastic comedies acted by the boy companies for the pleasure of the Court. Robert Greene, writing for the populace of London, was offering romance, in a blend of pseudo-history, magic, and love-story. Thomas Kyd had written the most renowned of English plays, *The Spanish Tragedy*, which popularized the Senecan features of the revenge motif, a high-flown rhetorical style, ruthless, cunning villains, and a general slaughter for the climax. Greene, George Peele, and many lesser playwrights were producing crude "chronicle" plays from English history, mingled with broad comedy.

We cannot be absolutely sure, but most scholars think it likely that Shakespeare's first produced plays were of the last-named genre, the "history" plays called the First, Second, and Third Parts of *Henry* VI. In general these are pedestrian in style and lack the imagination and artistry with which Shakespeare later dramatized the careers of English kings. In fact, his authorship of the *Henry* VI plays has been disputed; but their inclusion, by Heminge and Condell, in the

First Folio of 1623 (see Chapter 5) leaves little doubt
that they are mainly, if not wholly, by Shakespeare.
And it must have been during nearly the same years
that he composed his most "Senecan tragedy," the
crude melodramatic play of *Titus Andronicus*. It never
rivaled *The Spanish Tragedy* in popularity, however
much it tried to appeal to the same taste. Perhaps
about this time a tragedy of *Hamlet* by Kyd was
staged. A decade later Shakespeare was to make
Hamlet immortal and his tragedy the most famous of
dramas.

About 1588, perhaps about the same time Shakespeare came to London, an exciting new dramatist
began to write plays for the Lord Admiral's Company
— Christopher Marlowe. His *Tamburlaine*, Parts I and
II, *Dido, Queen of Carthage*, *The Jew of Malta*, *Dr.
Faustus*, and *Edward* II, all of which may have been
produced 1588-1592, gave to the English public and
playwrights a conception of beautiful blank verse and
powerful dramatic concentration which they had not
dreamed of before. Though both poets were born in
1564, Marlowe's genius had matured more rapidly than
Shakespeare's. But his literary career was cut short by
his employment in Secretary Walsingham's spy-system
and by his tragic death in 1593. Our uncertainty about
dates of production of both Marlowe's and Shakespeare's plays warns us to be cautious about asserting
his influence upon Shakespeare;[1] yet the traditional
view that *Richard* III (staged about 1592-93) owes
much to the example of Marlowe's concept of tragic
character and to his versification may be correct. The
dates of *Edward* II (1592?) and *Richard* II (about
1595) clearly permit a theory of Marlowe's influence;
and the parallels of theme and treatment give nearly

[1] Indeed, Prof. F. P. Wilson emphasizes Shakespeare's indi-
viduality and superiority in both comedy and history and inclines
to believe he may have preceded Marlowe as successful dramatist.
Marlowe and the Early Shakespeare, 1953, pp. 104-131.

everyone the impression that for Shakespeare *Edward* II pointed the way to a finer, more tragic kind of history play. Yet it is to be remembered that there are significant differences in Shakespeare's handling of the theme of the weak king. So engrossed did he become in the character and situation of Richard that he read more widely in preparing this play than he did for any other of his works[2] — a fact in itself enough to free him from any criticism of unworthy dependence on Marlowe. Furthermore *Richard* II became the basis of a series of three more plays on the Lancastrians who succeeded because of Richard's downfall.

Marlowe had no gift for comedy, whereas Shakespeare most decidedly had. However, as a young dramatist he found it easier to take his cue from earlier models than to invent a technique of his own. He had read Latin comedies at school and seen adaptations of them for the English stage; so he produced *The Comedy of Errors* on the plan of Plautus's *Menaechmi*. In *The Taming of the Shrew* he blended two strains of comedy, native English farce and Italianate intrigue borrowed from Gascoigne's *Supposes*, of which the source was Ariosto's *I Suppositi*. (Of course Italian dramatists also imitated Latin comedy.) Though in *Two Gentlemen of Verona* Shakespeare utilized situations from a Spanish romance, he probably borrowed them from an English play, rather than from the romance itself, Montemayor's *Diana*. *Love's Labour's Lost* is a comedy of witty play with words and literary styles; it has been thought to be a satire aimed at a clique of intellectuals who were more easily recognized by Elizabeth's courtiers than by today's audience. Certainly it appears to be a comedy designed for a sophisticated, courtly audience. In these respects it reminds one of Lyly's comedies, though it is by no means an imitation of any one of them. It pretends to tell of a contem-

[2] F. P. Wilson, "Shakespeare's Reading," *Shakespeare Survey*, III (1950), 18.

porary event, not a Greek myth, as so often Lyly does in his allegories. No printed source for *Love's Labour's Lost* has been found.

What has been said about these early plays may be summed up by the statement that for at least his first half dozen years in the theater, Shakespeare follows the patterns of contemporary genres — history play, farce, comedy of intrigue, tragedy — as he observed them in the London theaters. Though his imitation is certainly not servile, it is a following of successful formulas — unless we should except *Love's Labour's Lost*.

In 1592 and 1593 the bubonic plague, which ravaged London every few years, reached special severity, and as usual, the city government forbade public gatherings. This closing of the theaters was not unbroken; but the intermissions were not long enough to enable companies of actors to prosper. Like his fellow-actors, Shakespeare was probably in some financial distress. It may seem, therefore, not quite a coincidence that in 1593 he published an Ovidian narrative poem, *Venus and Adonis*. The goddess's love for a mortal youth is described in lusciously beautiful and sensuous style, only rivaled at times by that of Marlowe's similar work, *Hero and Leander*. Marlowe's poem was not yet printed, but it was probably circulating in manuscript in 1592. Thomas Lodge's Ovidian love-poem, *Glaucus and Scilla* (1589), certainly provided Shakespeare with some hints for the action of his narrative. *Venus and Adonis* is dedicated to the young Earl of Southampton and must have appealed to him, as it did to many other youths; it was said that university students sometimes slept with the book under their pillows. How much remuneration the sale of the manuscript to the publisher and the dedication to the Earl brought to the young poet, we do not know. Assuredly, this poem, its successor, *The Rape of Lucrece* (1594), and the sonnets (published in 1609, but well known in manuscript in the later 90's) established Master Shakespeare's reputation as a poet in his own generation. They brought him into friendship with the Earl of Southampton and probably into the circle of Southampton's friend, the Earl of Essex, Elizabeth's favorite. On the whole, Shakespeare made a brilliant advent in the literary world.

Indeed, we should be wrong to infer from the dates of the long poems that two hard years in the theater were the sole cause of his successful venture. On the contrary, many facts would justify us in believing that Shakespeare had dreamed of, and prepared for, his literary debut before he came to London. Like Marlowe, Chapman, and many others, Shakespeare no doubt aspired first to be a "poet" as distinguished from playwright. For English drama in the 1590's, as we learn from Sidney's *Defence of Poesie*, was regarded by literary people as hack work. How then do we explain the fact that after publishing *Lucrece* in 1594, Shakespeare devoted himself solely to play writing? No doubt the answer is in the man's character. Fame is admirable, but "solid pudding" is necessary; and Shakespeare had a family to support. There were plenty of examples in London to teach him that subsisting on the fruits of dedications to noblemen would mean hunger and debtors' prison. Shakespeare saw that a share in the Chamberlain's Company of actors could provide a good living for a man of his proved talents.

His concentration on writing highly ornamented narratives and possibly on the sonnets during this period of about 1590-1596 is reflected in several of the plays he wrote for his company during those years. Critics have spoken of this time as Shakespeare's lyrical period, and the term aptly suggests much of the literary style in *Love's Labour's Lost*, *A Midsummer Night's Dream*, *Richard* II, and *Romeo and Juliet*, all of which contain passages of beautiful description or lyrical emotion. The first two are also memorable for their charming songs. Sonnets are imbedded in *Love's Labour's Lost* and *Romeo and Juliet*. In all four plays the reader is conscious of the dramatist's intense interest in style, particularly in poetic devices. Shakespeare tries the effect of rhyme in sestains, quatrains, and couplets.

When the devout religion of mine eye	*a*
Maintains such falsehood, then turn tears to fires;	*b*
And these, who, often drown'd, could never die,	*a*
Transparent heretics, be burnt for liars!	*b*
One fairer than my love! The all-seeing sun	*c*
Ne'er saw her match since first the world begun.	*c*

(Romeo and Juliet, I. 2. 93-98.)

In this sestain the artificiality of the rhyme combines its effect with that of the absurd "conceit" (or fantastic metaphor) of tears described as religious martyrs burned for an heretical creed — "transparent heretics" ! But we are not disgusted by this artifice, for it presents Romeo, the affected lover of Rosaline, in an ironic light and is the foil to which his deeper lyrics of love for Juliet will later be contrasted. The artifice is therefore dramatic.

Besides rhyme patterns and conceits, Shakespeare uses devices of sound noticeably, such as alliteration, assonance, and consonants in patterns. In the second line of the preceding sestain note the alternation of *t* and *f* in stressed syllables. Note the vowels and consonants in these couplets:

Thou chid'st me well. Proud Bolingbroke, I come
To change blows with thee for our day of doom.
This ague fit of fear is over-blown;
An easy task it is to win our own.

(Richard ii, III. 2. 188-191.)

Line 1 rises to a climax in the sequence *ch, P, B, b, c.*
Line 2 is linked with line 1 by repetition of *ch* and *b*;
it mounts to the harsh climax of "*d*ay of *d*oom," as if
the emotional Richard had at last reached a pitch of
determination. But the last two lines by their melodious
vowel sounds, which grow lighter and lighter to the
end, and by their use of sibilant and liquid consonants
(*s, l, n*) unconsciously reveal the King's weakness and
prepare the audience for his fit of despair. Read the
lines aloud and listen to the sounds.

Rhetorical figures, such as climactic series, antithesis
of terms, and patterned speech in general, are not
poetic devices, strictly speaking. However, since they
are distinctive features of Shakespeare's narrative
poems and are abundant in the plays of the lyrical
period, they may be mentioned here. For an example,
take the lines

> Eyes, look your last!
> Arms, take your last embrace! and, lips, O you
> The doors of breath, seal with a righteous kiss
> A dateless bargain to engrossing death!
> Come, bitter conduct, come, unsavoury guide!
> Thou desperate pilot . . .
>
> (*Romeo and Juliet*, V. 3. 112-117.)

The figure of apostrophe is used in a climactic group
of three, *eyes, arms, lips;* but to prevent the triad from
being too mechanical, the last member is broken by a
phrase of description, *the doors of breath.* Another
triad follows, *righteous kiss, dateless bargain, engrossing death;* and still another (again, three apostrophes),
conduct, guide, and *pilot.* But the expected third instance of *come* is omitted and replaced by the con-
temptuous pronoun *Thou,* which sharpens the climax
of the hateful adjectives *bitter, unsavoury,* and *desperate.* (Death is unsavory because he inhabits stinking

charnel houses.) Obviously, the rhetorical patterns in these lines are emphatic. Note also the developing metaphor originated by *seal*, to press the warm wax on a document. A legal paper, a contract of a kiss to be exchanged for a death, is sealed by Romeo and Death; but it lacks a terminal date. There is also a pun in *engrossing*: Besides making ("engrossing") legal documents, Death is a monopolist ("engrosser") of all humanity.

Sometimes the result of these poetic and rhetorical devices is charming; seldom does the artifice jar upon the audience. But there are occasional serious lapses of taste. *Romeo and Juliet* has many lines of superb poetic beauty; but when Romeo, after slaying Tybalt, thinks of losing Juliet, he uses imagery that is bad:

More honourable state, more courtship lives

In carrion-flies than Romeo; they may seize

On the white wonder of dear Juliet's hand

And steal immortal blessing from her lips . . .

This may flies do, when I must from this fly.

(III. 3. 34-37, 41.)

Delighted with his phrase, "the white wonder," the poet perhaps did not clearly picture a girl's lips adorned with flies; and the final pun is inane. But it should be noted that *Richard* II and *A Midsummer Night's Dream* are free of such blunders, though they reveal just as clearly Shakespeare's absorption in poetic style.

Because this discussion of Shakespeare's style relates to his lyrical period, the student should not, of course, infer that in the earlier plays and the many greater ones to follow, these poetic and rhetorical devices are absent. A few minutes' examination of the plays will dispel that idea. In fact, the remarkable stage-success of *Richard* III throughout the centuries has been due to its powerful rhetoric as well as to its melodrama and its menacing hero-villain. Again, later plays like *Twelfth Night, As You Like It,* and *The Tempest* possess fine lyric passages and beautiful songs. However, in the histories, comedies, tragedies and romances that follow the lyrical period, Shakespeare's dramatic verse grows in subtlety and variety of technique, so that to a degree each play has its own style, while still sharing the maturity of power found in the others. In general, then, one may say that in the plays after about 1596 art has replaced artifice. The style has become so fully expressive of the thought that audience and readers are unconscious of the poet's devices. Nevertheless, analysis of passages will reveal their unobtrusive presence.

The middle and late 1590's mark Shakespeare's full success with the patterns of romantic comedy and of history play. By their charm of characterization (especially of women), dramatic skill, ironic humor, and eloquence of style, *The Merchant of Venice, Much Ado About Nothing,* and *As You Like It* have delighted audiences through the centuries. The group reaches its climax with *Twelfth Night.* These have been well called "the joyous comedies." One would infer that Shakespeare's prosperity with the Chamberlain's Men, his success as poet, England's relief from the threat of Spanish invasion, and the friendship of Essex and Southampton combined to foster Shakespeare's zest for comedy. But this easy inference should be qualified by the remembrance that his only son, aged eleven, died in 1596. We cannot know the spiritual experiences of the poet during these years.

Having tried, in *Richard* III, Marlowe's concentra-tration on one megalomaniac character, Shakespeare had painted in *Richard* II a sensitive, poetic figure of kingly weakness balanced by its inevitable counterpart, resolute opportunism in Bolingbroke. In both plays the only humor is an ironic light now and then thrown on tragic characters. But in a series of three plays (conceived as sequels to *Richard* II) Shakespeare now returned to an older fashion in the history play, a sequence of political events combined with comic episodes. Yet he so vastly improved the old-time formula that the two parts of *Henry* IV and *Henry* V are ranked as his supreme work in this genre. In the first place he viewed the political action from a philosophic standpoint and accordingly shaped characters and manipulated events in such a way as to intensify the drama without distorting the facts of history. Secondly, he not only organized the comic episodes into an action, but related this action to the political one in its significance as well as its movement of characters. To some degree, even, the comic characters are created to support the significance of the political plot. Falstaff and his bullies at the Boarshead Tavern constitute at least half the dramatic value of the *Henry* IV plays. However, having brought his hero, the young King Henry V, to the point of launching an attack on France which resulted in the glory of Agincourt, Shakespeare felt obliged to kill Falstaff, who despised glory. But a likely anecdote tells that Queen Elizabeth commanded his resuscitation, and that thereupon Shakespeare wrote him into *The Merry Wives of Windsor*, a farce that has remained popular.

Professor Mark Van Doren suggests that when Shakespeare came to write the third play on Prince Hal, *Henry* V, the dramatist became bored with his ideal soldier-king, his man of action who seemed to lack an interior life. This may be so; and it may also be true that in 1599 the English history play as a genre had gone out of fashion (excepting the tremendous popularity of the Falstaff plays). Whatever the reason, Shakespeare now turned to Roman history for a theme and a style for tragedy. As recent critics of *Julius Caesar* have said, if we dwell exclusively on Brutus's tragic failure, we may be ignoring the dominant political meaning of the play. Yet Shakespeare's concentration on Brutus and the fact that his character offers a parallel to Hamlet's seem to mark a new interest and power in Shakespeare's drama, a movement of his spirit that, in the years 1600-1606, created four of the world's greatest tragic dramas: *Hamlet, Othello, King Lear,* and *Macbeth.* His earlier tragedies of *Titus Andronicus* and *Romeo and Juliet* do not reveal a tragic perception of the mystery of evil or its effect on human character; it is only when we consider Richard II and Brutus as well as Shylock (in *The Merchant of Venice*) that we realize it was particularly the history plays which gave the dramatist his opportunity for preliminary sketches of tragic and potentially tragic heroes, as well as for meditation on the forces that control human destiny.

A nineteenth century critic, Edward Dowden, interpreted the four greater tragedies as signs of the deep anguish of Shakespeare's spirit over some personal disaster, and viewed them as cries "Out of the Depths." Although it is obvious that no writer could create these pictures of human anguish if he himself had not experienced profound misery at some time, we at once realize, also, that an unparalleled dramatic imagination is at work in these plays. Not only that; we have record of only two facts in Shakespeare's life which may be said to have caused him depression during these years: his disillusionment in the Earl of Essex, whose ambitions led to a treasonous revolt and death on the scaffold in 1601; and the death of Shakespeare's father in the same year. If there were other causes of despair, we do not know them. In 1601 Shakespeare was thirty-seven years old and even by Elizabethan standards, still near the prime of life. He was prospering, had purchased New Place in Stratford for his ultimate retirement, and, as a gentleman, had been granted a coat of arms. With the accession of King James I in 1603 (midway of the "tragic period") Shakespeare came under royal patronage as a "King's Man" and his plays were often presented at Court to the new sovereign, in whom, for a few years, all Englishmen had the highest hopes. It is true these hopes were largely disappointed; but even if the disillusion were an intensely personal matter to Shakespeare, which is unlikely, he could hardly have reached its depth until about 1606, the year in which he is found offering to the King (by birth a Scot) the elaborate compliment of a great play on a Scottish theme, *Macbeth*.

It is also worth noting that other dramatists were writing great tragedies during the first decade of the seventeenth century — Chapman, Jonson, Marston, and Tourneur, for instance. The revival of revenge tragedy is a notable feature in the first half of the decade. The vogue of verse satire may also indicate a degree of disillusion in the English outlook of this time. But without venturing further into generalizations, it is enough to say that we have no reason for assuming highly personal reasons for Shakespeare's creation of four successive masterpieces in tragedy.

As has been mentioned, verse satire became a literary fashion for two years after Joseph Hall's *Virgidemiarum* was published in 1597. Its object was vice and corruption among the denizens of a corrupt capital; its manner was violent invective. Its authors were the angry young men of the day; and perhaps feeling that they were enjoying too much the lewdness that they exposed, the Church, in 1599, forbade any further publication of satire. Thereupon John Marston, who had written two volumes, and Jonson, whose genius was satiric, transferred the spirit of verse satire and something of its invective and caricature to the stage. Satire and its natural auxiliary, harsh realism in depicting social life and character, became distinctive features of early seventeenth century comedy. (The influence of the private theaters upon this new mode is discussed in Chapter 2.)

Shakespeare's soul was too sympathetic to take

naturally to this kind of comedy. However, there are four plays which seem to show that he tried to adapt to it. Three of them have been called the "Problem Comedies" or "Bitter Comedies": *Troilus and Cressida, Measure for Measure,* and *All's Well That Ends Well.* The fourth is the strange tragedy of *Timon of Athens.* Only *Measure for Measure* has been dated with anything like precision, but all of them are likely to have been written between 1598 and 1608, that is, they fall in the same period as the great tragedies. But the chronology is not really so simple as that, for *All's Well* may be an earlier play rewritten, and *Timon* may have followed *Antony and Cleopatra* (1607), of which the poetic quality is infinitely more charming. For a generation at least criticism has raged about the meaning of *Troilus* and *Measure for Measure.* These are indeed problem comedies; but one premise in criticism ought to be that their author had in mind his audience's expectation of certain devices of satire. That Shakespeare's deep bitterness of soul originated these plays is not demonstrable and seems most improbable.

The two final Roman tragedies, *Coriolanus* and *Antony and Cleopatra,* differ greatly in mood, though they are comparable in uniform excellence of poetic eloquence and mastery of dramatic technique. Whether *Coriolanus* is essentially or only incidentally satiric is a current problem for critics; certainly its hero is presented with a detachment which strongly contrasts to Shakespeare's portrait of Antony. Antony and Cleopatra are drawn with superb poetic power and ironic humor, as if they were old favorites of Shakespeare's imagination.

The last fruits of Shakespeare's genius are the tragicomedies, or romances, of 1609-1612. Their relation to the special audience of the "private" Blackfriars theater is discussed in Chapter 2. The differences between Shakespeare's romances and earlier tragicomedies, such as *The Merchant of Venice* and *Much Ado*

About Nothing, are chiefly matters of tone or emphasis and style. The plot situations and dramatic devices are not very different. In the romances, for instance, the heroine may disguise herself as a man to seek for her lover or accompany him in flight from his enemies; but such disguise is also used in the earlier plays of *Two Gentlemen of Verona,* and *As You Like It,* and Portia and Nerissa assume men's roles (for a different purpose) in *The Merchant of Venice.* Again, the conflict of love for a woman with friendship for a man distresses the heroes of *Two Noble Kinsmen* (a collaborated play by Shakespeare and Fletcher about 1611); but this is also a theme of *Two Gentlemen of Verona* and *Much Ado.* However, in the romances the interest and emphasis are different. The dramatist exploits the distresses of the lovers at greater length and in a more fervid tone. The heroine of *Cymbeline,* Imogen, disguised as a page, wanders alone in the wilderness; is saved from starvation by her unrecognized brothers; unknowingly eats a drug that puts her in a trance; awakes to find a headless body, seemingly her husband's, beside her; takes service with a Roman general; sees her "husband's" body interred; takes part in a battle against her own countrymen; is struck by her husband, who is offended by the "page's" impertinence; and finally is united with her father the king, her brothers, and her husband. Thus disguise is used, not for light-hearted irony, but for many dramatic thrills: suspense for her safety, pity, admiration and triumph, as well as overtones of sadism and fear of incest. The dramatic possibilities of "boy-actor in role of woman disguised as youth" are exploited to the full. Furthermore, the villain's pretended debauching of Imogen is described to her husband with a lewdness found nowhere else in Shakespeare except *Othello.* But because *Cymbeline* is not tragic, the sexual imagery seems to serve no dramatic purpose.

In witnessing a romance, or tragicomedy, as written

by John Fletcher and other dramatists during the reigns of James I and Charles I, the courtly audience were made to luxuriate in the agonies and triumph of aristocratic lovers whose feelings of honor, love, and friendship have an unqualified intensity that is unrealistic (or "sentimental") and that is tested by situations of fantastic difficulty. The people of tragicomedy, whether they are good or bad, are of course never members of the lower or middle classes, who presumably are not capable of such ideals and sufferings. At the end, the cowardly, lustful, and treacherous persons are scornfully dismissed to exile; sometimes they demonstrate a sudden change of heart and are forgiven. If the hero has intrigued against the virtue of the heroine, his failure in that design and her love win his pardon. In summary statement, those are the elements of seventeenth century dramatic romance. By temperament Shakespeare was not capable of handling its themes without adding touches of humor. Hence not even *Cymbeline* is wholly in the mood of Beaumont and Fletcher's *Philaster*. And, except for *Cymbeline*, Shakespeare continued to provide a crew of comic characters who, though not so broad in their humor as Bottom, Launcelot Gobbo, or Sir Toby Belch, yet must have made strong appeal to the Globe audience. Such are Stephano, Trinculo, and Caliban in *The Tempest* and the old Shepherd, the Clown, and Autolycus in *The Winter's Tale*.

Fletcher has always been praised for the naturalness and wit of his gentlemen's dialogue; but it is not likely anyone would maintain that Shakespeare is really much inferior to him in this minor virtue. However, a more interesting comparison may be made between Shakespeare's latest verse and the peculiar fluency of Fletcher's blank verse, which possesses an easy flowing rhythm very near to the rhythm of everyday speech, yet constantly imbued with the heightening of meter. A hallmark of Fletcher's style is the use of feminine endings. Note the extra, unstressed syllables which end these lines:

I have begun a slaughter on my honor,
And I must end it there. — A sleeps. Good Heav-
ens!
Why give you peace to this untemperate beast,
That hath so long transgressed you? I must kill
him . . .

(*The Maid's Tragedy*, V. 1. 23-26.)

Shakespeare's verse, in his romances, also has abundance of feminine endings; and it is likely that this innovation (which he could also have observed in Middleton's and Massinger's style) influenced his own. However, Shakespeare's rhythm is more elastic and supple and his meaning more compressed than those of any other dramatist, including Fletcher. Some attempt to analyze these qualities is made in Chapter 5. Enough has been said here to suggest that Fletcher's influence on Shakespeare's themes and style is arguable, but impossible to prove decisively.

Setting apart questions of mutual influence, one finds in *Cymbeline*, *The Winter's Tale*, and *The Tempest* (especially in the latter two) an ease of technique and adroit showmanship which of course result from twenty or so years' experience in the theater, and which are offered with a smile (we may suppose) to the audience. Shakespeare's supreme confidence in achieving his effects is well justified by the sureness with which even minor characters are imagined and come alive, by the captivating music and power of the poetry, and by the delightful irony which suffuses most of the scenes. With such well-tested magic at his command, the dramatist continued to rely upon the venerable conventions of Elizabethan drama, such as the "chorus," disguise, exposition by First and Second

Gentlemen, and the cloak of invisibility. Fantastic and romantic as *The Winter's Tale* and *The Tempest* are in their stories, the dramatist's mellow understanding of human life makes these two of the most charming comedies ever written. These, the last works wholly his own, seem a proper farewell to the world of illusion he had explored so rewardingly.

5

Canon, Chronology, and Text

I

The *canon* of any writer is the list of works that are accepted by scholars as genuinely his own, in their entirety or in substantial part. An undergraduate is sometimes surprised to hear that there is any question about ascribing the authorship of a literary work to the proper writer. But in both early and more recent times, literary masters have left uncertainties about authorship by publishing anonymously. Commonplace examples in the nineteenth century were the journalistic publications of Mark Twain and Walt Whitman. To identify the writers of such unsigned pieces as their newspaper sketches and reviews, one needs an accumulation of various kinds of evidence. Because Shakespeare never supervised the publication of any of his plays and may even have been unaware that they were going to be published, we would expect to find that many of his plays were published anonymously, and that many anonymous plays are doubtfully ascribed to him. Fortunately, this is not so. The canon of his dramas has been almost entirely decided by an edition called the First Folio. But before discussing it, let us consider why many early English plays were in fact published anonymously.

To understand why, we need to know the conditions in which they were written. Inevitably, in the sixteenth century, which was the Renaissance in England, contemporary plays had to stand comparison with Greek and Roman drama. But the native traditions of culture and of convention in the theater had resulted in plays so different from the classics that for many years English plays were disparaged or rejected by the educated. There was another and better reason for anonymous publication. The actors had to have a large repertory and a constant supply of new plays. As a result play-writing became, in large part, hack-writing, and much of the product was trash. It was natural, therefore, that few professional poets cared to have their names attached to plays or wished to become known as play "botchers" (i.e., patchers). However, by the 1590's a change of attitude had begun. The power of genius — Lyly's, Marlowe's, Shakespeare's, and Jonson's — was beginning to be recognized by literary critics. Above all, in the year of Shakespeare's death, 1616, his friend and rival, Jonson, greatly helped to destroy the critical prejudice by publishing his own plays in a folio edition entitled *The Works of Benjamin Jonson.* True, Jonson considered himself a classicist, his plays show certain influences of classic drama, and he perhaps felt justified on that ground. But Jonson was also thoroughly independent and English. Possibly, if he had not defied the sneers of critics by publishing the folio of his *Works,* Shakespeare's fellow-actors might not have had the courage to edit his plays in the First Folio of 1623 — and many of his plays would have been lost for ever.

But two of his old associates, John Heminge and William Condell, esteemed him as man and poet so much that they undertook the work. Their big book of the plays at once fixed the canon of Shakespeare's works, with the exception of a few for which Shakespeare had had some responsibility, but was not sole author. One of these, *Pericles,* is now always included in "the complete works"; another, *The Two Noble Kinsmen,* sometimes has been. There is far less complete agreement about *Edward* III and *Sir Thomas More*. Incidentally, most scholars agree that John Fletcher, a younger playwright, was the other author who collaborated with Shakespeare on *The Two Noble Kinsmen* and *Henry* VIII. From time to time other anonymous plays have been ascribed to Shakespeare, but never with the full assent of many scholars and critics. On the other hand, a few scholars have doubted that the three plays called *Henry* VI (though they are in the Folio) are wholly by Shakespeare; but in general the trilogy is accepted as his. The standard canon of Shakespeare today, then, includes the thirty-six plays of the Folio plus *Pericles*, a total of thirty-seven. Thomas Heywood, a popular dramatist of that era, asserted that he had written, or shared in the writing of, over 200 plays, of which less than 50 were printed. Thomas Dekker, another popular writer, is known to have had a hand in 75 and probably many more, in the course of thirty or thirty-five years at work. Of Dekker's output, 17 were printed. Assuming that few or none of Shakespeare's plays have been lost, his average output over twenty or twenty-five years' time is less than two plays per year. We may infer, therefore, that Shakespeare was a steady, but not unusually prolific, contributor to his company's repertory, and that his works were valued and carefully preserved by the company.

II

The term *chronology*, as applied to the plays, ordinarily means 'the dates at which they were *produced*.' Production presumably followed *composition* within a few weeks or months; so that they must usually have been close to the same date. *Publication*, however, ordinarily followed long after production — at least twenty-nine years later for *A Comedy of Errors*. Scholars have generally believed, probably rightly, that the actor-owners tried to prevent publication of plays, at least those of a popular dramatist like Shakespeare, whose works would usually attract customers to the theater through several revivals. Nevertheless, other men's plays sometimes reached print within a year or two of production. The various ways in which a manuscript might reach a printer's hands will be suggested below, in the section on "Text." Our primary interest, which is in Shakespeare's developing art, leads us to concentrate here on the date of composition and production.

In attempting to date, at least approximately, the composition of each of Shakespeare's plays, scholars make use of several kinds of facts, classified as *a*] "external" and *b*] "internal" evidence.

a] External evidence is usually, but not always, stronger. It includes records of production or publication. Publication, of course, furnishes a "downward limit" for dating, that is, a "latest possible" date; but as was mentioned in the last paragraph, this limit is often of small use. Consider, for instance, that the First Folio was published more than seven years after Shakespeare's death, and that of the 36 plays in it, 18 had not been published before. Actually, all of the 18 were at least eleven years old (for the dramatist ceased to write about 1612), and most of them were much older. Publication, then, is not often close enough to fix the date of composition precisely.

There is another form of external evidence that is of more help: This is a reference to the play in a work of literary criticism, a letter, a diary, or other record. For instance, Francis Meres, a clergyman in his early thirties living in London in 1597-1598, wrote an enthusiastic, but pedantic, little book of criticism, called *Palladis Tamia*. In the course of evaluating the leading writers of England, he praises Shakespeare and enumerates twelve plays, probably all that he knew of by that writer.

His list serves both positively and negatively. Clearly

it furnishes a downward limit of composition for the twelve plays. But it is fully as useful in its omissions; for several plays which, on other evidence, we should think Shakespeare wrote between 1597-1600, are not mentioned by Meres and therefore almost certainly were not produced until after he had published his book, late in 1598. Among these are *Much Ado* and *As You Like It*.

Another form of record, incomplete, but still surviving in part, was made by the Master of the Revels. This official was primarily charged with arranging the forms of entertainment for the monarch and Court on festival occasions. His records of payment for performances at Court have, for some plays, the importance of being a first mention and fix a downward limit of composition and first production. A Court performance of *Othello* on November 1, 1604, recorded by the Revel's office, must have been a very early production, if not the first, of that play, which on other grounds also seems to belong to 1604. Occasional records of productions also occur in the diaries of John Manningham and Simon Forman, which help to date *Twelfth Night*, *Cymbeline*, and *The Winter's Tale*.

b] The internal evidence for date is found within the play itself. Allusions to well known events or notorious personages may indicate the date of composition, for such references usually have interest for the audience only for a short time, after which they may be replaced by other news. In *A Midsummer Night's Dream* the prominent reference to a disastrously wet year that ruined crops has been accepted by most scholars as a "topical reference" to 1594 and 1595; and presumably Shakespeare wrote the play within a few months or a year or two at most after the bad weather, that is, in 1595. In *The Merry Wives of Windsor* there is a joke aimed at a German prince who had made himself objectionable on a recent visit in England. When scholars today agree in finding an allusion to a contemporary person or event of interest to Shakespeare's audience, the allusion may well have value in dating. However, we know that new topical references, particularly in comedy, were sometimes added to plays on later revivals, perhaps to replace outdated references. For this reason they cannot in general be viewed as conclusive evidence of date.

Another type of internal evidence lies in the use of source materials. Shakespeare is notorious for having borrowed his plots. Unfortunately, his habit is not often useful in dating the composition, for he usually went back to an old book, Holinshed's *Chronicles*, 1587, Belleforest's *Histoires Tragiques*, 1582, North's *Plutarch*, 1595, or Greene's *Pandosto*, 1588. But not always. In *King Lear* he took, not the plot, which was old, but devil-lore, from Harsnett's *Detection of Popish Impostures*, published in 1603. Between this date and the record of performance on December 26, 1606, he seems to have composed the tragedy.

Still another minor form of internal evidence is the presence of echoes — that is, repetitions of allusion, phraseology, or theme. For instance, Macbeth says, in III. 1. 54-57, ". . . . Under him, / My Genius is rebuked; as, it is said, / Mark Antony's was by Caesar." In *Antony and Cleopatra*, a soothsayer tells Antony of his inferior spirit and Antony confirms the truth of it, the interview making most of the substance of the third scene of Act II. One would infer that these two plays were composed at times not far distant from each other, though the coincidence by itself does not establish the priority of either. The coincidence can only be used to support stronger indications of chronology. Because picturesque references to Tarquin's rape of Lucrece occur in *Macbeth*, II. 1. 55, and in *Cymbeline*, II. 2. 12, we cannot, on that account, make any useful inference about chronology. Long before, Shakespeare had written his poem *The Rape of Lucrece*, published in 1594, and the story of Tarquin seems often to have come to his mind.

Finally, there is the internal evidence of style. Several kinds of data may be considered under the head of style. A leading one is the "regularity" of the verse. Blank verse, the prevailing verse of Shakespearean drama, is composed of five-beat lines in which an unstressed syllable is followed by a stressed one, so that the total is ten syllables to the line, as in the following:

For ere thou canst report I will be there,
The thunder of our cannon shall be heard.
So hence! Be thou the trumpet of our wrath
And sullen presage of your own decay.

(*King John*, I. 1. 25-28.)

If dramatists kept strictly to the fundamental pattern of this iambic pentameter line, the rhythm would soon grow intolerably monotonous. But, in fact, the sense of the words and phrases hardly allows an unvarying following of this rhythm. And in reality the dramatist aims at much more subtle and moving rhythms of speech. Though the audience in the theater do not consciously analyze these subtle changes in the rhythm, students may have various reasons for doing so. When they do, they find that as Shakespeare grew more and more practiced as a writer of dramatic verse, he made the rhythm more elastic, more subtly captivating, by introducing various devices. It is impossible to illustrate all these changes fully without giving great space to the matter. Here we shall only notice a few devices that Shakespeare came to employ more and more:

1] Substitution of trochaic (/x) or spondaic (//) feet for iambic feet, thus:

Now might I do it pat, now he is praying.

Now might and *now he* may be interpreted as trochees (/x).

$$\acute{}\quad\acute{}\quad\acute{}\quad\acute{}_{\times}\quad\acute{}\quad_{\times}\acute{}\quad_{\times}\acute{}$$

Yare, yare, good Iras; quick. Methinks I hear

Yare, yare and *good I-* are spondees ($//$).

2] Use of run-on lines, that is, lines in which
the sentence continues from one verse line to the next
without marked pause:

Give me my robe, put on my crown; I have
Immortal longings in me. Now no more . . .

There can be no long pause between subject and verb
or verb and complement. Hence, the effect of the "run-
ning on" between *have* and *immortal longings* is really
to unite the iambic pentameter lines into a larger rhyth-
mic pattern.

3] Greater variety in the strength and position of the caesuras, or pauses, within the iambic line
and at its end. The five-beat line has a tendency to fall
into two parts, separated by a slight pause; for instance, into two beats, then three; or into one beat, then
four; or into some other division. In Shakespeare's
earlier writing the interior caesura is light, unnotice-
able, and not very significant in rhythmical pattern:

Perhaps some merchant | hath invited him
And from the mart | he's somewhere gone to dinner.
Good sister, | let us dine and never fret.
A man is master | of his liberty.

(*A Comedy of Errors*, II. 1. 4-7.)

In his later plays the caesuras become much varied in
position and strength, so that they are important aux-
iliaries of the rhythm:

Beseech you, sir, | be merry; || you have cause,
So have we all, | of joy; || for our escape

Is much beyond our loss. || Our hint of woe
Is common; || every day some sailor's wife,
The masters of some merchant,[1] | and the merchant
Have just our theme of woe . . .

> (*The Tempest*, II. 1. 1-6.)

A little study of several verse passages should convince the student that 2] and 3] above are but different
aspects of the same matter, that is, that run-on lines
and varied caesuras introduce a second principle of
rhythm into the blank verse, to contrast to, and also to
support, the iambic pattern at the base. It is, in fact, a
principle of syncopation; the rhythm of speech, the
freer rhythm of cadence, operates in the lines to
heighten our appreciation of the iambic meter. The
phrases and clauses of speech can take on a rhythm of
their own, and perhaps always do so.

4] Use of the feminine ending. This is an eleventh
syllable, unstressed and added to the end of the line:

Now might I do it pat, now he is praying.

> (*Hamlet*, III. 3. 73.)

In contrast, the basic iambic pentameter is masculine,
and this, of course, is the predominant form in Shakespeare's earlier verse:

Good sister, let us dine and never fret.

> (*A Comedy of Errors*, II. 1. 6.)

Last to be mentioned in these changing aspects of
style is the *compression* that must be noted in Shakespeare's later utterance:

> How you speak!

Did you but know the city's usuries,
And felt them knowingly; the art o'th'court,

---

[1] Merchant means 'merchantman,' vessel.

As hard to leave as keep, whose top to climb
Is certain falling, or so slippery that
The fear's as bad as falling; the toil o'th'war
A pain that only seems to seek out danger
I'th' name of fame and honour which dies i'th'
        search,
And hath as oft a slanderous epitaph
As record of fair act; nay, many times,
Doth ill deserve by doing well . . .

                        (*Cymbeline*, III. 3. 44-54.)

In such a passage as this, the compression is, first, and
obviously, in the suppression of parts of syllables in
prepositions and articles (*o'th'court*) by which three
syllables become two. More importantly, the connec-
tives are suppressed (". . . knowingly, [as well as]
the art o'th'court, [which is] as hard to leave as [it is]
to keep [and] whose top . . ."). Furthermore the
words now have great pregnancy of meaning. In this
passage *knowingly* has, not a single meaning, but a
double. It is a pun meaning both 'by experience' and
'cunningly.' *Leave* means 'to part from' and 'give up as
a bad job.' *Keep* means to 'retain' and also to 'keep in
high practice.' And so on.

These various aspects of style, then, enable critics
and scholars to see a progression among the plays and
to assign them tentatively to early, middle, or late
periods in Shakespeare's development. But style, like
other forms of internal evidence, serves best to support
external evidence or stronger internal evidence. It is
possible for anyone to discover passages in the early
plays which in style approximate very nearly to the
qualities which have been cited above as representing
Shakespeare's mature and his final periods. Nevertheless, style has validity as a clue to chronology.

III

The matter of *text* was introduced earlier in this chapter in speaking of the publication of the First Folio as the principal source of the canon. The undergraduate student should understand the special sense which the word *text* carries in the following paragraphs. In general, a text is any printed version or any manuscript of a human discourse. A "good" or "sound" or "authentic" text of a Shakespeare play is one which comes close to, or perhaps quite attains, the language, punctuation, and even spelling which Shakespeare intended it to have. Invariably, then, one uses the word *text* with the connotation of 'accurate version,' 'version close to what Shakespeare actually put on paper.' You may be surprised to learn that there is any difficulty about knowing what Shakespeare actually wrote — but only if you have forgotten how hard it is for you to copy a selection of just a few lines with perfect exactness. The copyists whose versions (and changes) intervened between Shakespeare's final draft of his plays and your anthology of them may have been all or some of these persons: 1] A scribe who prepared the promptbook and other "parts" for the King's Men, copying from Shakespeare's papers; 2] a scribe who copied the promptbook for the printers; 3] the compositor, or typesetter, who transferred the manuscript to type; 4] editors, from the eighteenth century on, who have "improved" or "corrected" the first editions; and 5] modern compositors who re-set the first editions. In spite of great reverence for Shakespeare's genius, there is ample room for error in all these transmissions! And we have not even mentioned that a fluent writer like Shakespeare must have left unquestionable errors in his own final draft.

Before outlining the relations among early texts of Shakespeare, it is necessary to distinguish two terms used in library science and analytical bibliography:

folio and *quarto*. They are now used primarily to refer
to the size of books. Today, as in Shakespeare's time, a
folio is the largest size of book. In making a folio in the
seventeenth century, the printer printed two pages on
each side of a standard sheet of paper. Then, for binding
into the finished book, the sheet was folded once and thus
furnished two large leaves, that is, four pages.[2]
Folios were too large to carry around or hold in the
hands while reading; they required a table or a book
rack. Such large volumes were used for Bibles, sermons,
theology, history, natural science, and philosophy.
Learning and dignity marked the folio; and we understand Ben Jonson's audacity in publishing his mere
plays as his *Works* in folio.

Nowadays *quartos* are decidedly large books; but in
Shakespeare's time they were smaller and measured in
the neighborhood of seven inches wide by ten long. In
making a quarto book, the printer printed four pages
on each side of the *unfolded* sheet; and the binder folded
each sheet twice, before inserting it as a gathering into
the book. The first gathering carried pages 1-8, the
next pages 9-16, and so on. A quarto was then a port-
able size of book; and a quarto of a single play, which
rarely ran to many more than eighty pages, was small
enough and thin enough to be carried in a capacious
pocket. As play quartos left the bookseller's shop almost
always in paper wrappers, not hard covers, it is not
surprising that only a few copies of such editions have
lasted to the present day.

Because the plays in the First Folio of Shakespeare
were prepared for the press by the dramatist's good
friends and associates, Heminge and Condell, the texts
in the Folio must be regarded as of high authority.
"High," indeed, but not always the *highest* authority;
for nineteen of the plays had been published in quarto,

[2] For stronger binding the Shakespeare Folio was printed and
sewed "in sixes." Three printed sheets were laid together and
folded once into a *quire* of six leaves. Many quires make the book.

as single editions, before the Folio came out, and some were used as copy by the printers of the Folio. Certain of these editions may even approach more closely to the manuscript Shakespeare offered to the actors as "fair copy" (final draft) than do the Folio texts. Some scholars have believed that a few quarto editions were set in type directly from the author's manuscript. On the other hand, it is very likely that most of the Folio texts were set by the printer from scribal copies of Shakespeare's manuscripts.

How did the manuscripts used for the quarto editions come into the hands of the printers and publishers? We do not know; the answer must be a speculation. But it seems safe to say that, with one possible exception, Shakespeare himself never instigated the publication of any of his plays. The possible exception is the Second Quarto of *Hamlet*. In 1603 appeared a garbled and corrupt edition of the play, now called the First, or "Bad Quarto," perhaps written out by an actor who had had a minor part or parts in the play not long before. He remembered his own lines almost perfectly, of course; but his memory of the remainder of the lines was fragmentary and blundering. However, a publisher of little scruples was willing to pay the actor for the manuscript, and a printer was found for it. It is believable that Shakespeare saw this maimed version of his play somewhere, and in disgust asked the King's Men for permission to publish a better text. Apparently they gave this permission for the printing of a long and very authentic text, called the Second, or "Good," Quarto, 1604.

However, one fact seems clear, that Shakespeare never supervised the printing of any of his plays, not even this good quarto of *Hamlet*. Too many obscurities and errors remain in it to allow the supposition that the author corrected the proof.

The speculations on how other of his plays reached quarto editions must be solved by study of each text.

Even within the Folio, marked differences of form indicate different kinds of manuscripts in the printers' hands. Some manuscripts may have been scribal copies of the promptbook of the play. Others may have been copies of Shakespeare's final draft, which had been deposited in the files of the King's Men. Still others may have been transcriptions assembled from the parts distributed among the actors. Similar diversity may be assumed for the manuscripts of the quarto editions. Now, given these various kinds of copies, one may speculate rather freely about how the manuscripts passed from the actors to the publishers. Rarely is there any genuine evidence in the matter.

The most challenging early editions are six "bad quartos," those of *Henry* vi, Part ii and Part iii, *Romeo and Juliet, Henry* v, *Hamlet*, and *The Merry Wives of Windsor*. They are bad in different degrees; and for them also, the problem of origin is a complicated one. Sometimes a company that had been on tour outside of London broke up, and sold its plays to publishers. Such versions were often shortened ones. Another theory has been advanced to account for "bad quartos," that of theft (or "piracy") of plays by means of stenographic copies made in the theater during performance. But more popular today, and probably more sound, is the theory of "memorial reconstruction." A "traitor actor," out of employment and in need of cash, perhaps with several former members of his company, sits down and reconstructs the play from memory, as well as he and his mates can; then he offers it to a publisher.

All manuscripts to be printed of any kind whatsoever were supposed first to be read and licensed by the deputy of the Bishop of London and one of the wardens of the guild of printers and booksellers called the Stationers' Company. One would expect that a very corrupt text would cause one of these licensers to ask the publisher embarrassing questions and so perhaps discover the fraud. But ordinarily a play was not an extremely valuable literary property, and hence if unscrupulous publishers sometimes failed to observe the law about licensing, by publishing a play without registering it, chances were fair of escaping detection and fines. Yet two of the bad quartos — *Henry* vi, Part ii, and *The Merry Wives of Windsor* — were actually registered before publication, though they are very corrupt texts. The publishers may not have inquired closely about the origin of the manuscripts; and the publishers were not challenged by the licensers.

So it is that for some of Shakespeare's plays we have two texts, a good quarto and the Folio; and for others, three, or more, a bad quarto, a good quarto (or several such) and the Folio. The variations among these texts are both interesting and important. An illustration of them is found in the texts of *Hamlet*, which may be merely sketched as follows: The Bad Quarto is about 1700 lines shorter than the "received" text usually found in our anthologies today; but besides this defect, it is garbled and corrupt in its wording, and there are notable changes in the action. Yet occasionally it throws light on the diction and especially on the staging, in the more authentic texts. The Second (Good) Quarto is the longest single version of the three original ones, and by many scholars it has been thought to have been printed from a manuscript in Shakespeare's handwriting. The Second Quarto contains about 218 lines absent from the Folio version; yet it lacks about 85 found in the Folio. These are the larger differences. Scores of individual variants, consisting of single words and differences in stage directions, distinguish these two authentic texts.

One cannot blame the bewildered student who may now ask, "But which is the real *Hamlet*?" Seeking for the answer, scholars try to establish the true text by study of all the variants from good and bad texts, with the purpose of finding out how the variations arose. First, all the variants must be listed; next they must be compared, and a reason must be discovered for each difference. In this analysis scholars try to apply all the available knowledge of Elizabethan handwriting, Shakespeare's diction as found in sound texts of other plays, theater customs, and printing practices. From this intensive study they hope to construct a theory of the origin of each text, and in the light of that theory, to choose rightly among the variants. The process is too arduous for many editors. In practice, therefore, they often combine the Second Quarto and Folio versions of *Hamlet*, supplying from one what is lacking in the other, except where the two conflict. Then a choice must be made which, again, should be based on the editor's theory of the origin and authenticity of the texts.

For instance of combination (or "conflation"), in Act I, Scene 1, in the Second Quarto, Bernardo and Horatio speak the lines commonly numbered 108-125. They are not found in the Folio; but anthologies which reprint the Folio version usually give these lines from the Quarto, sometimes in square brackets. Conversely, in Act II, Scene 2, lines 244-276, as usually given, are found in the Folio, not in the Quarto. They will not be in brackets if the Folio is the basic text adopted. Now for an instance of conflict, take the celebrated word in line 129 of I. 2:

Oh that this too too solid Flesh, would melt . . .

Solid is the Folio reading, *sallied* is the Quarto reading. *Sallied* comes from a very authentic text and cannot easily be set aside as a blunder by either Shakespeare or a scribe. But perhaps in Shakespeare's handwriting, the *u* of *sullied* looked like an *a*, and the printers erred in setting an *a* for a *u*. This view may be supported by a study of other *a-for-u* errors in the texts of *Hamlet* and other plays. If enough of them occur, *sullied* would appear to be the authentic reading.

Such conflicting variants may ultimately be solved by scholars' exhaustive effort. Less hopeful are the dark obscurities, or *cruxes*, that occur singly in one text or the other, or even in both. For example, the Folio, at I. 1. 63, reads:

He smot[e] the sledded Pollax on the Ice.

The Second Quarto reads *sleaded pollax*. Edmund Malone was the first to emend *pollax* to *Polacks*, a form now dialectal, but in Shakespeare's time standard English, meaning 'Poles.' The whole phrase, therefore, means "He struck the Poles, who ride in sledges on their icy rivers."

Emendation is the substitution of words to achieve a meaning of some sort in a passage which the changes of language or the blunders of scribe or printer have left in complete obscurity, unilluminated by the best efforts of linguists, paleographers, bibliographers, and other scholars. Emendation, said Dr. Samuel Johnson, "demands more than humanity possesses, and he that exercises it with the most praise has very frequent need of indulgence."

In the textual notes in your version of the plays, F_1 denotes the First Folio, Q_1 and Q_2 the first and second quartos. A Second Folio was published in 1632, a Third in 1663, and a Fourth in 1685; but they are reprints from the first and have so little textual authority that the undergraduate need pay little attention to them. However, they testify to Shakespeare's popularity and prestige. The series of all the Folios is denoted by *Ff*, of all the quartos of a given play by *Qq*.

6

A Chronology of Literature and Events, 1557-1616

THE FOLLOWING LISTS begin seven years before Shakespeare's birth, with the publication of Tottel's Miscellany, an anthology of major importance in the development of Elizabethan poetry. They end with the year of Shakespeare's death.

The student should note that the items in Columns II and III are highly selective. As "important literary works" only those books are cited which Shakespeare probably read, or which strongly influenced English poetry or drama, or which seem to the compiler to signalize changes in literary taste. But Shakespeare's reading was by no means confined to the works listed in Column II. And only *first editions* are noted in Column II; actually, Shakespeare must often have read and used later editions of these books.

In Column I the date for each play is the supposed date of *first production*. Though question marks are not used here, the student must remember that these dates are usually conjectural (see Chapter 5). Dates of the poems are, however, those of publication.

For the items in Columns II and III the compiler owes much guidance to similar lists by two scholars, C. S. Lewis, in *English Literature in the Sixteenth Century Excluding Drama* (Oxford, 1954), and Douglas Bush, in *English Literature in the Earlier Seventeenth Century 1600-1660* (Oxford, 1945).

I	II	III
Production of Shakespeare's Plays.	*Important Literary Works of Shakespeare's Age.*	*Important Historical Events of Shakespeare's Age.*
	1557. Richard Tottel, *Songs and Sonnets* (Tottel's Miscellany).	1557. The Stationers' Company is chartered.
		1558. Accession of Queen Elizabeth.
	1559. William Baldwin, *Mirror for Magistrates* (enlarged edition).	
	1559-60. Jasper Heywood trans.[1] Seneca, *Tragedies.*	
1561. Production of *Gorboduc,* first English Senecan tragedy.		1561. O'Neill's rebellion in Ireland.
	1562. Arthur Brooke, *Romeus and Juliet* (poem). Richard Grafton, *Abridgment of the Chronicles of England.*	
		1563. The Thirty-Nine Articles promulgated.
		1564. Birth of Shakespeare, Marlowe, and Galileo.
	1565. *Jests of Skoggan.* John Stow, *Summary of English Chronicles.*	

[1] *Trans.* of course means 'translates.'

I	II	III
Production of Shakespeare's Plays.	*Important Literary Works of Shakespeare's Age.*	*Important Historical Events of Shakespeare's Age.*

1566. Arthur Golding trans. Ovid, *Metamorphoses*. Production of George Gascoigne, *The Supposes*.

1566-67. William Painter, *The Palace of Pleasure*.

1567. Anonymous, *Merry Tales by John Skelton*. Geoffrey Fenton, *Tragical Discourses*. George Turberville trans. Ovid, *Heroical Epistles*.

1567. Revolt of the Netherlands against Spain.

1568. Sir Thomas North trans. A. Guevara, *The Dial of Princes*. The Bishops' Bible.

1568. Mary Q. of Scots flees to England. Elizabeth seizes a Spanish treasure fleet.

1569. Thomas Newton trans. Cicero, *Paradoxes of the Stoics* and *Of Old Age*.

1569. Rebellion of the Northern Earls.

1570. Bishop John Leslie writes *The History of Scotland*. A. Ortelius, *Theatrum Orbis Terrarum* (in Antwerp).

1570. The Pope excommunicates and deposes Elizabeth.

1571. The Battle of Lepanto.

1572. R. H. trans. Lavater, *Of Ghosts and Spirits*.

1572. The Massacre of St. Bartholomew. Society of Antiquaries is founded. Birth of John Donne.

I	II	III
Production of Shakespeare's Plays.	*Important Literary Works of Shakespeare's Age.*	*Important Historical Events of Shakespeare's Age.*

	1573. Gascoigne, *A Hundreth Sundry Flowers.*	
		1574-75. Persecution of Catholics and Anabaptists in England.
	1576. *Paradise of Dainty Devices* (anthology of verse). George Pettie, *Petite Palace of Pettie His Pleasure.*	1576. The Theatre built in London.
	1577. Raphael Holinshed, *Chronicles.* Richard Eden, *History of Travel in the Indies.*	1577. The Curtain and Blackfriars theaters open in London.
		1577-78. Drake's voyage around the world.
	1578. John Lyly, *Euphues, the Anatomy of Wit.* George Whetstone, *Promos and Cassandra.*	
	1579. North trans. Plutarch, *Lives.* Edmund Spenser, *The Shepherd's Calendar.* Stephen Gosson, *The School of Abuse.*	1579. The Jesuits sent to England.
	1580. Stow, *Chronicles of England.* Belleforest, *Histoires Tragiques.* M. de Montaigne, *Essais,* I-II.	

I	II	III
Production of Shakespeare's Plays.	*Important Literary Works of Shakespeare's Age.*	*Important Historical Events of Shakespeare's Age.*

	1580-84. Sir Philip Sidney writes *The Defence of Poesie.*	
	1581. Arthur Hall trans. Homer, *Iliad,* I-IX. Barnabe Rich, *Farewell to Militarie Profession.* John Studley and others trans. *Seneca his Ten Tragedies.*	1581. Negotiations for the marriage of Elizabeth to the Duke of Anjou.
	1582. Richard Hakluyt, *Voyages.* *New Testament,* Rheims version (Catholic). Richard Stanyhurst, trans. Virgil, *Aeneid,* I-IV. Thomas Watson, *Hekatompathia* (sonnets).	1583. Irish rebellion. Two English plots suppressed.
	1584. Production of Lyly, *Campaspe* and *Sapho and Phao.* Reginald Scott, *Discovery of Witchcraft.*	1585. English expeditions against the Spaniards in the Netherlands and Spain under Leicester and Drake respectively.
1586. Production of Thomas Kyd, *The Spanish Tragedy.* William Webbe, *Discourse of English Poetrie.*		1586. Death of Sir Philip Sidney. Censorship of the press established. The Babington Plot.

I	II	III
Production of Shakespeare's Plays.	*Important Literary Works of Shakespeare's Age.*	*Important Historical Events of Shakespeare's Age.*

	William Warner, *Albion's England.* William Camden, *Britannia.*	
	1587. Production of Christopher Marlowe, *Tamburlaine,* Parts I and II. Angell Day trans. Longus, *Daphnis and Chloe.* In Italy, C. Monteverdi's first book of madrigals.	1587. Execution of Mary Q. of Scots. Drake attacks Cadiz.
	1588. Production of Lyly, *Galathea* and *Endimion,* and of Marlowe, *The Jew of Malta.* Robert Greene, *Pandosto.* William Byrd, *Psalmes, Sonets, and Songs.*	1588. Defeat of the Spanish Armada. Death of the Earl of Leicester.
	1588-89. Production of Marlowe, *Dr. Faustus,* and of Greene, *Friar Bacon and Friar Bungay.*	
1589-90 1 *Henry* VI; *Titus Andronicus.*	1589. Thomas Lodge, *Glaucus and Scilla.* George Puttenham, *Art of English Poesy.*	1589. Civil war in France.
1590-91 2 and 3 *Henry* VI.	1590. Production of Greene, *James* IV, and of Lyly, *Midas.* Lodge, *Rosalynd.* Sidney, *Arcadia* (in part).	1590. Death of Sir Francis Walsingham.

I	II	III
Production of Shakespeare's Plays.	*Important Literary Works of Shakespeare's Age.*	*Important Historical Events of Shakespeare's Age.*

	Spenser, *The Faerie Queene,* I-III. Watson, *First Set of Madrigals Englished.* Anthony Munday trans. *Amadis of Gaul.*	
	1591. Production of Greene, *Orlando Furioso.* Sir John Harington trans. Ariosto, *Orlando Furioso.* Sidney, *Astrophel and Stella.* King James VI of Scotland, *Poetical Exercises.* Sir Henry Savile trans. Tacitus, *Histories.*	1591. Expedition against the Spanish in the Azores.
1592-93 *Comedy of Errors* and *Richard* III.	1592. Production of Marlowe, *Edward* II. Samuel Daniel, *Delia* (sonnets) and *Complaint of Rosamond* (tragic narrative). Henry Constable, *Diana* (sonnets). Greene, *Groatsworth of Wit* (contains an attack on Shakespeare). Thomas Nashe, *Pierce Penniless.*	1592. The plague in London. The Rose theater opened. Death of Greene.
1593 *Venus and Adonis.*	1593. Henry Chettle, *Kind Heart's Dream* (contains a compliment to Shakespeare).	1593. The plague in London. Death of Marlowe. Heavier penalties for recusancy.
1593-94 *The Taming of the Shrew: Two*	Michael Drayton, *Idea* (sonnets).	

I	II	III
Production of Shakespeare's Plays.	*Important Literary Works of Shakespeare's Age.*	*Important Historical Events of Shakespeare's Age.*

Gentlemen of Verona.	Lodge, *Phillis* (sonnets). Barnabe Barnes, *Parthenophil* (sonnets). Richard Hooker, *The Laws of Ecclesiastical Polity.*	
1594 *The Rape of Lucrece.*	1594. Thomas Morley, *Madrigals to Four Voices.* Nashe, *The Unfortunate Traveler.* Anonymous, *Zepheria* (sonnets).	1594. Wet weather, poor harvests. Death of Kyd.
1594-95 *Love's Labour's Lost; Romeo and Juliet.*		
1595-96 *Richard II; Midsummer Night's Dream.*	1595. Daniel, *The Civil Wars.* Sidney, *The Defence of Poesie.* Spenser, *Amoretti* (sonnets). Drayton, *Endimion and Phoebe.*	1595(?) Building of the Swan theater. Raleigh's voyage to Guiana.
1596-97 *King John* and *The Merchant of Venice.*	1596. *Spenser, The Faerie Queene,* IV-VI. Sir Walter Raleigh, *Discovery of Guiana.* Bartholomew Griffin, *Fidessa* (sonnets). Thomas Deloney, *Jack of Newbury.*	1596. The Earl of Essex victoriously storms Cadiz. Spain sends aid to the Irish rebels.

I	II	III
Production of Shakespeare's Plays.	*Important Literary Works of Shakespeare's Age.*	*Important Historical Events of Shakespeare's Age.*

1597-98

1 and 2 *Henry IV.*	1597. Joseph Hall, *Virgidemiarum.* Deloney, *The Gentle Craft.* King James VI of Scotland, *Demonologie.* Sir Francis Bacon, *Essays.* Robert Tofte, *Laura* (sonnets). Drayton, *England's Heroical Epistles.*	1597. Failure of Essex's expedition against Spain's treasure fleet.

1598-99

Much Ado About Nothing and *Henry* v.	1598. Production of Ben Jonson, *Every Man in His Humour.* George Chapman trans. Homer, *Iliad,* I-VII. Marlowe, *Hero and Leander* (completed by Chapman). Thomas Speght edits Chaucer, *Works.* John Marston, *Pygmalion* and *Certain Satires.* William Rankins, *Seven Satires.* Francis Meres, *Palladis Tamia.* Bartholomew Young trans. Montemayor, *Diana.* Thomas Grenewey trans. Tacitus, *Annals.*	1598. The Edict of Nantes. Death of Sir Robert Cecil, Lord Burghley. The Earl of Tyrone defeats the English in Ireland. The Theatre is torn down and its timbers used to build the Globe.

1599-1600

As You Like It and *Julius Caesar.*	1599. Marston, *The Scourge of Villainy.* Thomas Middleton, *Micro-cynicon.*	1599. A Spanish expedition to aid the Irish frustrated by storms. The Earl of

I	II	III
Production of Shakespeare's Plays.	*Important Literary Works of Shakespeare's Age.*	*Im ortant Historical Events of Shakespeare's Age.*
	John Weever, *Epigrams.* Production of Jonson, *Every Man Out of His Humour* and of Marston, *Antonio and Mellida.* Sir John Hayward, *Life of Henry* IV. *The Passionate Pilgrim* (anthology containing two of Shakespeare's sonnets).	Essex, sent as Lord Deputy to Ireland, returns without permission and is imprisoned in his house. The Globe theater opens. Death of Spenser.
1600-01 *The Merry Wives of Windsor, Twelfth Night,* and *Hamlet.*	1600. Sir John Davies, *Epigrams.* Sir William Cornwallis, *Essays.* Nicholas Breton, *Melancholic Humours.* Marlowe, *All Ovid's Elegies.* *England's Helicon* (anthology). Philemon Holland trans. Livy, *Roman History.*	1600. The Fortune theater opens. East India Company founded.
1601-02 *Troilus and Cressida.*	1601. Jonson's and Marston's plays in the "Stage Quarrel." John Chamber, *Treatise Against Judicial Astrology.* Philip Rosseter and Thomas Campion, *A Book of Airs.* Thomas Wright, *Passions of the Mind.* Holland trans. Pliny, *Natural History.*	1601. Insurrection and execution of Essex. English victory in Ireland. Siege of Ostend begins.
1602-03 *All's Well That Ends Well.*	1602. Simon Patericke trans. I, Gentillet,	

I	II	III
Production of Shakespeare's Plays.	*Important Literary Works of Shakespeare's Age.*	*Important Historical Events of Shakespeare's Age.*

I	II	III
	Against Niccolo Macchiavel. John Brereton, *Discovery of the North Part of Virginia.* Campion, *The Art of English Poesy.* Francis Davison, *A Poetical Rhapsody* (anthology).	
	1603. John Florio trans. Montaigne, *Essays.* Holland trans. Plutarch, *Morals.* Production of Jonson, *Sejanus.* Richard Knolles, *General History of the Turks.* Daniel, *Defence of Rhyme.* Drayton, *The Barons' Wars.*	1603. Death of Elizabeth and accession of James VI of Scotland as James I of England. English conquest of Ireland. Plague in London. Two plots against James suppressed. Imprisonment of Raleigh for treason.
1604-05 *Measure for Measure* and *Othello.*	1604. Production of Thomas Dekker and Middleton *The Honest Whore,* Part I, and of Marston, *The Dutch Courtesan.* Bacon, *His Apology Concerning the Late Earl of Essex.* Sir William Alexander, *Monarchic Tragedies.*	1604. Peace with Spain. The Hampton Court Conference frustrates the Puritan clergy. End of the siege of Ostend.
1605 *King Lear.*	1605. Production of Jonson, Chapman, and Marston, *Eastward Hoe!* and of Jonson's first masque,	1605. Repression of Puritans and Catholics. The Gunpowder Plot discovered.

I	II	III
Production of Shakespeare's Plays.	*Important Literary Works of Shakespeare's Age.*	*Important Historical Events of Shakespeare's Age.*

	The Masque of Blackness. Bacon, *The Advancement of Learning.* Joshua Sylvester trans. S. du Bartas, *Divine Weeks and Works.*	
1606 *Macbeth.*	1606. Production of Jonson, *Volpone.* Holland trans. Suetonius, *The Twelve Caesars.*	1606. New penalties against recusants. Charter for Virginia. Visit of the King of Denmark.
1606-07 *Antony and Cleopatra.*	Drayton, *Poems Lyric and Pastoral.* Dekker, *Seven Deadly Sins of London.* Production of *The Revenger's Tragedy.*	
1607-08 *Timon of Athens* and *Coriolanus.*	1607. Production of Francis Beaumont, *The Knight of the Burning Pestle.* King James, *Apology for the Oath of Allegiance.* Edward Grimeston trans. J. de Serres, *General Inventory of the History of France.*	1607. The King imposes bishops on the Scottish Church. Founding of Jamestown. Trouble in Ireland.
1608 *Pericles.*	1608. Joseph Hall, *Characters of Virtues and Vices.* Captain John Smith, *A True Relation of Virginia.* Production of Chapman, *Conspiracy of Biron* and *Tragedy of Biron,* and	1608. A league with the Dutch. The Separatists move to Holland. Birth of John Milton.

I	II	III
Production of Shakespeare's Plays.	*Important Literary Works of Shakespeare's Age.*	*Important Historical Events of Shakespeare's Age.*

	of Beaumont and John Fletcher, *Cupid's Revenge.*	
1609 *Sonnets* and *A Lover's Complaint.*	1609. Production of Jonson, *Epicoene,* and of Beaumont and Fletcher, *Philaster.* Fulke Greville, *Mustapha.*	1609. The commissioners for Virginia are shipwrecked in Bermuda. The King's Men begin to play in the Blackfriars theater.
1609-10 *Cymbeline.*	1609-10. *Old Testament,* Douay Version (Catholic).	
1610-11 *The Winter's Tale.*	1610. Silvester Jourdain, *A Discovery of the Bermudas.* William Strachey, *The Wreck upon the Bermudas.* Production of Jonson, *The Alchemist.* John Healey trans. St. Augustine, *The City of God.*	1610. The plantation of Ulster begins. Henry IV of France murdered.
1611-12 *The Tempest.*	1611. *The King James Bible.* Thomas Coryate, *Coryate's Crudities.* John Donne, *Ignatius his Conclave.* Production of Jonson, *Catiline his Conspiracy,* and of Beaumont and Fletcher, *The Maid's Tragedy* and *A King and No King.*	1611. The Court of High Commission is given greater power over the clergy. Conflict with the Dutch.

I	II	III
Production of Shakespeare's Plays.	*Important Literary Works of Shakespeare's Age.*	*Important Historical Events of Shakespeare's Age.*

1612-13

Henry VIII and *The Two Noble Kinsmen* (both partly by Fletcher).

1612. Drayton, *Poly-Olbion,* I-XVIII.
Thomas Heywood, *An Apology for Actors.*
Thomas Shelton trans. Cervantes, *Don Quixote,* Part I.
Daniel, *History of England,* I.
Chapman trans. Homer, *Iliad,* I-XXIV.
Production of John Webster, *The White Devil.*

1612. Burning of witches in Lancashire. Death of Prince Henry. England's alliance with German princes.

1613. William Browne, *Britannia's Pastorals,* I.
George Wither, *Abuses Stript and Whipt.*
Sir Henry Spelman, *De non temerandis ecclesiis.*
Beaumont, *Masque of the Inner Temple.*

1613. Marriage of Princess Elizabeth to the Count Palatine of the Rhine. Murder of Sir Thomas Overbury in the Tower of London. The Globe theater burns.

1613-14. Production of Webster, *The Duchess of Malfy.*

1614. Production of Jonson, *Bartholomew Fair.*
Lodge trans. *Works of Seneca.*
Raleigh, *The History of the World.*
John Napier, *Logarithmorum Descriptio.*
Sir Thomas Overbury, *Characters.*

1614. Parliament protests against James I's taxation and is dissolved. Benevolences are imposed. Negotiations begun for Prince Charles's marriage to the Spanish Infanta.

1614-15. Chapman trans. Homer, *Odyssey,* I-XXIV.

I	II	III
Production of Shakespeare's Plays.	*Important Literary Works of Shakespeare's Age.*	*Important Historical Events of Shakespeare's Age.*

	1615. Production of Jonson, *Mercury Vindicated,* and Daniel, *Hymen's Triumph* (masques). Wither, *Shepherd's Hunting.* Camden, *Annales,* I. Breton, *Characters upon Essays.*	1615. James i visits Cambridge University. Negotiations with the Dutch over trade in the East Indies.
	1616. Chapman trans. *The Divine Poem of Musaeus.* First Folio edition of *The Works of Benjamin Jonson.* Healey trans. Theophrastus, *Characters.* King James i, *works,* Captain John Smith, *Description of New England.*	1616. Death of Shakespeare and Cervantes. Trial of the Earl and Countess of Somerset for the murder of Overbury. Rise of Villiers, later Duke of Buckingham. Yielding of the cautionary towns to the Dutch.

The Publication of Shakespeare's Plays and Poems

IN THE FIRST of the following lists the plays are arranged in the assumed order of their production (see "Chronology," Chapter 5, for the difficulties of dating them). Single editions of the plays are indicated by dates; they are not distinguished as quarto or octavo editions, but most of them are quartos. The dates of the successive folio, or collected, editions of the plays in one volume are these: Folio$_1$, 1623; Folio$_2$, 1632; Folio$_3$, 1663; and Folio$_4$, 1685. "Folios" after a play means that the play was printed in all four.

Please note that editions after 1623, whether quarto or folio, are reprints and have almost no textual value. They are cited here merely to indicate Shakespeare's popularity in the seventeenth century.

In the second list the plays are arranged in the order of their first appearance in print.

i IN ORDER OF PRODUCTION

Probable Date of Production

1589 - 90	Part I *Henry* VI. Folios.
1589 - 90	*Titus Andronicus.* 1594, 1600, 1611; Folios.
1590 - 91	Part II *Henry* VI. (Bad quartos under title *The First Part of the Contention of the Two Famous Houses of York and Lancaster*) 1594, 1600, 1619; Folios.

*Probable
Date of
Production*

1590 - 91	Part III *Henry* VI. (Bad quartos under the title *The True Tragedy of Richard Duke of York and the Death of Good King Henry the Sixth*) 1595, 1600, 1619; Folios.
1592 - 93	*The Comedy of Errors.* Folios.
1592 - 93	*Richard* III. 1597, 1598, 1602, 1605, 1612, 1622, 1629, 1634; Folios.
1593	*Venus and Adonis.* 1593, 1594, 1595(?), 1596, 1599 (two editions), 1602(?), 1607 (1608?), 1608 (1609?), 1610(?), 1617, 1620, 1627, 1630(?), 1630, 1636, 1675.
1593 - 94	*The Taming of the Shrew.* (Under the title *The Taming of a Shrew*—the authorship of this play has been disputed), 1594, 1596, 1607; (as *The Taming of the Shrew*) 1631, Folios.
1594	*The Rape of Lucrece.* 1594, 1598, 1600 (two editions), 1607, 1616, 1624, 1632, 1655.
1593 - 94	*Two Gentlemen of Verona.* Folios.
1594 - 95	*Love's Labour's Lost.* 1598, 1631; Folios.
1594 - 95	*Romeo and Juliet.* 1597 (a bad quarto), 1599, 1609, 16—(?), 1637; Folios.
1595 - 96	*Richard* II. 1597, 1598 (two editions), 1608, 1615, 1634; Folios.
1595 - 96	*A Midsummer Night's Dream.* 1600, 1619; Folios.
1596 - 97	*King John.* Folios.
1596 - 97	*The Merchant of Venice.* 1600, 1619, 1637; Folios.
1597 - 98	Part I *Henry* IV. 15—(?), 1598, 1599, 1604, 1608, 1613, 1622, 1632, 1639; Folios.
1597 - 98	Part II *Henry* IV. 1600; Folios.
1598 - 99	*Much Ado About Nothing.* 1600; Folios.
1598 - 99	*Henry* v. (Bad quartos) 1600, 1602, 1619; Folios.
1599 - 1600	*Julius Caesar.* 1684, 1691 and four undated quartos from the late seventeenth century; Folios.
1599 - 1600	*As You Like It.* Folios.
1600 - 01	*The Merry Wives of Windsor.* (The first two are bad quartos.) 1602, 1619, 1630; Folios.
1600 - 01	*Twelfth Night.* Folios.
1600 - 01	*Hamlet.* 1603 (a bad quarto), 1604-05, 1611, 16—(?), 1637, 1676, 1676(?), 1683, 1695; Folios.
1601 - 02	*Troilus and Cressida.* 1609; Folios.
1602 - 03	*All's Well That Ends Well.* Folios.
1604 - 05	*Measure for Measure.* Folios.
1604 - 05	*Othello.* 1622, 1630, 1655, 1681, 1687, 1695; Folios.

*Probable
Date of
Production*

1605	*King Lear.* 1608, 1619, 1655; Folios.
1606	*Macbeth.* 1673; Folios.
1606 - 07	*Antony and Cleopatra.* Folios.
1607 - 08	*Timon of Athens.* Folios.
1607 - 08	*Coriolanus.* Folios.
1608	*Pericles, Prince of Tyre.* 1609 (two editions), 1611, 1619, 1630, 1635; Folio₃, Folio₄.
1609	*The Sonnets.* 1609, 1640.
1609 - 10	*Cymbeline.* Folios.
1610 - 11	*The Winter's Tale.* Folios.
1611 - 12	*The Tempest.* Folios.
1612 - 13	*Henry* VIII. Folios.
1612 - 13	*The Two Noble Kinsmen.* 1634, 1679 (in Beaumont and Fletcher, *Fifty Comedies and Tragedies*).

ii IN ORDER OF PRINTING

1593	*Venus and Adonis.*
1594	*The Rape of Lucrece.*
1594	Part II *Henry* VI, *Titus Andronicus. The Taming of a Shrew* (see the note in preceding list).
1595	Part III *Henry* VI.
1597	*Richard* II. *Richard* III. *Romeo and Juliet.*
1598	Part I *Henry* IV. *Love's Labour's Lost.*
1600	*Henry* V. Part II *Henry* IV. *Much Ado About Nothing. A Midsummer Night's Dream. The Merchant of Venice.*
1602	*The Merry Wives of Windsor.*
1603	*Hamlet.*
1608	*King Lear.*
1609	*Troilus and Cressida. Pericles, Prince of Tyre.*
1609	*The Sonnets.*
1622	*Othello.*
1623	In Folio₁ all the preceding plays except *Pericles,* as well as the following ones: *Two Gentlemen of Verona, The Comedy of Errors, As You Like It, Twelfth Night, Measure for Measure, All's Well That Ends Well, Cymbeline, The Winter's Tale, The Tempest, King John,* Part I *Henry* VI, *Henry* VIII, *Julius Caesar, Timon of Athens, Macbeth, Antony and Cleopatra, Coriolanus.*
1634	*The Two Noble Kinsmen.*

Index

NOT ALL INSTANCES of the word *Shakespeare* in the text are cited here, but a considerable number of topics are classified under the dramatist's name. All of the titles of Shakespeare's and other dramatists' plays have been indexed, but names of characters from the plays have not. However, it may prove helpful that when a character is discussed in the text, the title of the play is cited in the index. Historical events and persons, as enumerated in the chronology in Chapter 6, are in general not indexed.

114